About the Author

I believe that it is not by chance that I am an aspiring author born exactly on Balkan lands. I have always been interested in the mysterious, restlessly analysing the deep underlying meanings behind everything and everyone. I have always lived close to nature, which has gifted me with a breath of fresh reasoning — far away from the loud background noise and unclean energy of the big city. I have two Master's degrees — one in Linguistics and one in Psychology. I have studied both fields extensively throughout my whole life; while gathering evidence for the real language of the soul and for our true unmasked nature, in a pragmatic and systematic way. All of this, and much more, has led me to write this book during my short breaks in between full-time work, studying, adventures, travelling and problem solving.

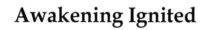

Awakening Ignited

R. P. Heaven

Awakening Ignited

Olympia Publishers
London

A CIP catalogue record for this title is
available from the British Library.

ISBN: 978-1-80074-081-5

First Published in 2021

Olympia Publishers
Tallis House
2 Tallis Street
London
EC4Y 0AB

Printed in Great Britain

Dedication

Dedicated to my soulmate and better half, who somehow
managed to turn my single sparkle into a glowing star.

A MESSAGE FROM THE AUTHOR

I am a human being just like you. I was born here, and I had to go through my inner and outer challenges to discover the Truth. My belief is that we all share a similar experience in that; and upon profound introspection we could all reach one core truth — the Truth with a capital "T". I know that some things are universally right and universally wrong; and all it takes to distinguish one from the other is to look for this knowledge on the inside.

I was born on a mystical ground. The Bulgarian lands are known for producing old souls encoded with profound truths. Bulgaria has been the motherland of many prominent mystics, psychics, visionaries, spiritual leaders, diviners and prophecy tellers — back in ancient times and up to this point. The Balkan Mountains exist on a higher frequency, and this can be seen in our traditions — and folklore music in particular. Its specific rhythms match the beats of the heart and have been proven to benefit both the blood circulation and general health. There is something more to it, however.

It has been over forty-four years since a Bulgarian folk song was launched into space on NASA's Voyager 1. The Golden Record, including "Izleel e Delyo Haidutin" performed by the folk artist Valya Balkanska, is still travelling through space to this day. It was not by chance that this particular Bulgarian piece was chosen. There is something to Balkanska's song, which brings a mood of forgotten knowledge and nostalgia for home — for our real home, that is. It is hard to put into words, but it can be felt.

Bulgarian souls are known for having gone through fathomless hardships; but also, for being unyielding in spite of that. It is almost as if we had an intrinsic knowledge of how to defy all odds, cope with evil, and stay in the Light. Bulgarian spirit remained unbreakable even after five centuries of Ottoman slavery and numerous other external predicaments and malevolent influences that continue to this day.

Perhaps, I have picked up nothing but a single sparkle from that ancient Bulgarian spirit; from the collective mind and genome of my ancestors — of all the unyielding warriors, enlightened mystics, visionary artists and inventive intellectuals. This single sparkle will be handed down to my next of kin, so that this strong Balkan tradition will live on with every next generation after me — just as it has lived on for millennia.

However, I want to share this exclusive light with you too. It has been my mere reason to look within for answers as I have always known it shines somewhere in there, although faintly at times, waiting to be fully ignited. I want to openly invite you to take from this vital flame and use it for good. Remember that it represents one unified ever-relevant truth; and it is the universal key to all doors — the door to happiness, peace, love, balance and purity. It is the key to knowing God and yourself.

It is the key to awakening.

"Do not look for happiness outside yourself. The awakened seek happiness inside." — Peter Deunov (Beinsa Douno) — Bulgarian philosopher, mystic and visionary.

IGNITION PHASE I
BALANCE

THE TRUTH IS

"At times you have to leave the city of your comfort and go into the wilderness of your intuition. What you'll discover will be wonderful. What you will discover is yourself." — Alan Alda

I need you to know the Truth.

Hopefully, you can take a single sparkle out of my story and light the path of your own journey.

I am writing mainly for those who appreciate abstract expression, imagination and the big picture. For those who choose not to see the trees for the forest. The different ones. The ones who lack interest in the petty things. The ones who prefer empathy and balance over cold logic and rationality. The ones who just know that there is something beyond our physical existence and don't need physical proof for it. The ones whose souls ache for having to exist only on the surface.

I don't know about you, but my heart is in pain every time I don't find meaning. I feel as if I am wasting away if I don't see the big reason behind things. I don't need details; I don't need physical science or statistics, as they are limited. But I do need to listen to my own inner compass to tell me right from wrong, and to guide me in my decisions — that Voice which is always there to lead me. I have ignored it in the past and have gone towards the wrong path that is not MY path, always aware that I am cheating my own nature.

"Do not be conformed to this world, but be transformed

by the renewal of your mind, that by testing you may discern what is the will of God, what is good and acceptable and perfect." — Romans 12:2

You see, I rely on my intuition. The Voice with a capital "V" that I just mentioned. It is the most powerful tool ever, and yet it is hard to manage, hard to explain, and hard to utilise for the little things like statistics or cold logic. But you don't really need it for that.

The Voice is revealing to you the greater truth behind things, the essence of our reality. You don't need to know every little detail of this reality; you are not allowed to, either. But yet there are some of us who are born with this additional sense; with this gift of abstract revelation which goes beyond human logic and the rationality of this world. That is why it is so hard to explain, and to manage. I believe you are one of those people and it's not by chance that you picked this book.

"Our bodies have five senses: touch, smell, taste, sight, hearing. But not to be overlooked are the senses of our souls: intuition, peace, foresight, trust, empathy. The differences between people lie in their use of these senses; most people don't know anything about the inner senses while a few people rely on them just as they rely on their physical senses, and in fact probably even more." — C. JoyBell C

The Voice, or intuition, comes with its requirements for expression, so that other people too could gain from the exclusive truth. This expression is inevitable, and you can't hold it in. It's like holding down the need to cry. You can suppress it for so long, but sooner or later, you will burst out.

My first desire to write a book hit me like a lightning bolt back when I was nine. It was such a powerful and exciting feeling that I did not know how to define it or where it came from. I just had to write. I guess I have always been wiser for my age because of this Voice, and I didn't need to read a lot of books in order to be aware of how to put it into practice.

Naturally, I made an attempt back then. Wrote about seventy pages, manually. Not all that bad either — I actually found it later at the age of seventeen while I was looking for something else, having forgotten about it. I felt I had met an old friend — my own better self — as I was reading through my scattered writings. My teenage years were somewhat chaotic and unsound, and getting to read this felt like decoding an important message from my past self who was not smarter, but in some odd ways was more stable, and pure. Unlike my writings now, my novel attempt back then was fictional — fantasy, mystery, drama, all that. But surely, with a subliminal philosophical truth.

That particular book tells the story of a boy who after a tragic event in his family spontaneously goes into another dimension, or into the past, or into his own mind, or it is all a dream — this was supposed to be revealed only at the end, which I never reached. But you must have your own theory here, and I am sure you are right.

In my head, this other world had different colours — not exactly black and white but definitely less saturated and gloomier, with dirtier shades. Similar to that "sepia tone" filter in photography. Exploring this new world, the boy finds a hidden castle. He goes into this castle; everything is dark and creepy, as it should be, of course (doesn't it remind you of the unconscious realm?)

… and then he finds… himself. Both metaphorically, and physically.

To be more precise, he finds his doppelgänger — the

same- looking boy who is actually the only one from this other world or dimension that can see and communicate with him. When the shock phase ends (after all they look exactly the same), they spend a lot of time together getting to know each other and sharing their heartaches from their family dramas and traumas, as new obstacles come their way.

Even though they look the same and have had similar experiences, they seem to have very different coping mechanisms and expressions in the outer world. Our main character is sensitive but aloof, hurting, piling everything inside so that others don't suffer. Holding everything in and putting up walls is his choice of defence. The other boy has the same sensitive traits, but pain has piled up in him, so he acts more openly and harshly, in anger, and in nervous and loud self- protection. Putting everything out and choosing to attack is his defence mechanism.

What they do share is a mission — to bring light and peace within their communities and the closest people around them, who live in anger and pain, who live in the shadows. And this is how each of the boys grows, getting to know the other more, and attuning his own inner compass influenced by the other. Neither is universally right. Neither is the chosen one. And yet they both are.

Change is not the easiest and most flawless thing — on the contrary. In the process of their evolution, whether it is through play, exploring, or simply talking, they fight a lot. They experience bitterness and frustration; and they have a hard time breaking down walls, letting go of ego and old beliefs.

Thanks to this conflict the two boys do not just help each other grow up, they gradually begin to bring each other out from the shadows, and that is why their encounter is fateful. They fight, they laugh, they cry together, they aid and complement one another. Sometimes they get in the way of each other, whether it is on purpose or not. It is a constant dance of lights and shadows, going back and forth.

However, reaching the end of my writing, thanks to their interaction and relentless seeking, it appears that they have begun to understand the Light and the Truth of things, and they have started to work together as a faithful team — as One; getting closer to the image of a single graceful sage, who has acknowledged and understood his inevitable darkness, and has put it to good use.

***

Going back now and having to write about it, I wonder if this was my nine-year-old self's metaphorical attempt to explain the journey we have with our own inner selves in the process of growing up and becoming brighter and wiser individuals.

Knowing one's own shadow is the first step of turning it into a light.

But you have to never stop seeking and comparing the two; you have to be fearless and let them dance. Where there is movement, there is change. This evolution of the Inner Self and the great Source's aid in that have always been my favourite topics of introspection and conversation with others who share similar beliefs to mine.

My theory is that the Inner Self, along with its demands for outer expression and growth, gains constant knowledge from the great Source, also known as God, through this channel which I call the Voice with a capital "V", or intuition.

However, during this complex and beautiful growth, the individual encounters inner and outer obstacles; and has to overcome them all.

"Every challenge of the human self-expands the divinity of the higher self." — Anthon St Maarten

The biggest challenge is to overcome your own dark side. However, this is the only first step of achieving balance. Many people just don't want to go out of the shadows — they feel cosy there. It is their comfort zone. There is no movement; no dance of lights and shadows. And while their souls go still every day, their Voice grows weaker with every next choice they make to only exist on the surface, without gradually exploring the Deep, or the unconscious realm. I imagine the Voice like a channel, or a ray of light directly flowing from above down into your body; and those people's rays thin out more and more with each wrong choice they make — until in the end there is nothing, and they have cut out their own connection with God.

I wonder what it would be like if I actually finished the book back then — would I have come up with a great realisation and a philosophical truth that would help my peers and family finally awake to the Truth and explore the Deep? I doubt it. It was too early for me back then. Maybe that's why I left it unfinished, and I also left unfinished writings multiple times after that. Even though I had the need to write, it was just too early, and I wasn't ready. My God, I am still unsure if it is not too early for me now. I guess we will have to see, judging by the prospect if I will bring this big stream of consciousness to the end.

"You either have to write or you shouldn't be writing. That's all." — Joss Whedon

I need to give freely what was given to me. I wish for everyone to use their tools in their own ultimate ways, in order to fulfil their own missions. Because at the end of the day, all of us have different missions; but the essence of our nature and the meaning of our existence is the same. Everyone deserves to be happy and wise. Following the thread of this knowledge over the years, a whole lot of things have changed around me, and within me; but this striving for creation and expression has always lingered inside me, waiting to be unlocked and set free for everyone to access.

The thing I am most proud of in my existence is that I have enriched my ray of light over the years, this channel which directly flows into me from the Source; the Voice in me has become louder and stronger, uncompromising to the obvious lies, as well as the lies masterfully disguised as truths. I am a believer in God now more than ever, and my connection with him has yet to become even stronger. And this has manifested in the quality of my relationships, and overall quality of life.

Of course, I am not always right — I can't be, after all I am just a human. Errare humanum est. But I know that my strength and my knowledge come not from me and my own ego, but from what lies beyond me — from the Source, from its great Light, and from the Voice with which I was gifted. The most powerful tool which is hard to explain, and to manage. But it gives you the Truth — nothing more, nothing less — only if you listen closely, and if you are ready to explore the Deep, namely your own unconscious realm.

"The Kingdom of Heaven is within." — Luke 17:21

YOU HAVE TO LISTEN

I have not always listened closely. In fact, there was a time in my life in which I blocked this pure light because I chose to live in the shadows for a while. The most reckless thing to do, but nonetheless part of my journey, and of my inner battle. Just like the two boys in my old writing, I danced back and forth with my shadows and lights in order to find myself, letting the shadows take the lead for a while and forgetting that I was never truly lost. My nine-year-old self's book attempt reminded me later on, just at the right time at seventeen.

But jumping back at an earlier point in my life — I was fourteen and I had my first existential crisis. I just didn't know who I was "supposed" to be. I was away from home for the first time, having just begun high school and studying in another city. I lived with three other girls in the same dorm room, which was old, mouldy and no bigger than eighteen square metres including a tiny bathroom with a sliding door. We slept on bunk beds and we had this huge table which took the majority of space in the room. I had no space, nor privacy. I guess none of us did, but the others seemed to take it better than me.

I guess I have always been an introverted person, but this was just a huge leap for me. Having grown up as a single child, without brothers or sisters, I had always appreciated my own space and felt safe and calm in it. I had never been lonely or afraid to be left alone with my thoughts, on the contrary. I had this vivid imagination which I interacted with on a daily basis, and most of the time I would find it far more interesting than playing with my peers, who always seemed too "childish" to me. There were times in which I would invent my own creative games or roleplays, being too bored of the standard ones which just seemed too easy, or too meaningless. I kept playing them regardless, so that I could be part of something; so that I could be accepted by my peers.

Trying to be accepted is what kept me calm, at least in the beginning, in this dorm situation as well. It wasn't meaningless that I didn't have my own space: I had found my reason, and I clenched onto it. For the first time ever, I tried really hard to be accepted; harder than I should have. It's not that the three other girls were all that bad; it's just that they were different. Or I was different. They always seemed united and I was the odd one out, no matter how hard I tried to be like them, and to be liked by them. I had the same experience in my class — I never seemed to fit in any of the cliques. I always appeared awkward, insecure, strange, clumsy, too sensitive or too careless; inauthentic. I was seeking my way in the dark, bumping ceaselessly in my blind attempts.

I felt as if my own personality was changing shades, or even as if I had no personality. I was a blank canvas and I let everyone paint their own shadows onto me freely. With what was left from my intuition, I must have grasped the symbolism of it. This must be the explanation why when we were all asked by our literature teacher, "What animal do you identify with?" I answered "chameleon".

At the back of my mind, I always knew that by allowing myself to be influenced by others in order to be accepted, I was cheating my own nature. But I couldn't care less — I just didn't like myself back then and thought I deserved it anyway. What I didn't realise at the time was very simple. I had just stopped listening to the Voice. And what I didn't like about me was not my true whole Self, but my prevailing shadow. It was just that part of me which I didn't like.

I had let external factors get a hold of me. And since I had no space or time for self-reflection and cleansing from other people's energies, I just stopped doing it. I took everything from the outside in, trying to adapt to it in order to be accepted. I never truly expressed my truths from the inside out. I didn't take the time to breathe, slow down a bit, and listen to my inner voice, as I would just go on and on for what seemed like ages.

I never made any drama, I didn't even cry. I didn't have the spatial intimacy to do so, even if I wanted. I just felt numb. I know now that this was my choice. I surely had the strength in me, and the Voice had always been there to freely give me wisdom and warm support. But at this time, I chose to ignore it on such a heavy number of occasions that it became blurry, distant and later on — deactivated. At the age of fifteen, for the first time ever, I felt lonely in my own company. I made the habit of ignoring my intuition and I was left to my own devices...

Being left to your own devices is a choice. It's not a turn of events, as there is not a single tragedy in your life which could force you to silence the Voice and cut your connection with the Source. Intentionally silencing the Voice is also the beginning of a series of catastrophes which could manifest in some, or all, aspects of life — physical health, mental health and authenticity, relationships, finance, overall wellbeing.

Cutting the connection can cause severe damages to your life, including addictions and substance abuse, gambling, fetishes, sexual deviations and perversions, induced psychiatric disorders, self-harm and harm to others. It could result in devastating repercussions like crime, rape, murder and suicide in the most severe cases.

In other words, when you choose to silence the Voice and cut your connection with the Source, preventing the Light from flowing through you freely, you gradually get used to living in the shadows. It becomes your natural habitat; it becomes your comfort zone. This is why some people find it so hard to escape their own vicious cycles, and prefer to stay there and complain, or put the blame on others. The victim state is directly related to that.

In that sense, hurting yourself and others could become a habit like any other. Just like pouring that first glass of alcohol first thing in the evening after another day of dissatisfying work. When you cease the flow of light, shadows slowly but surely crawl their own way into your mind and nest comfortably there. And since you don't allow the light in and there is no dance or movement, the shadows become the norm and you slowly forget that there is another half of you too, which you readily neglect: your pure light.

"A man who is possessed by his shadow is always standing in his own light and falling into his own traps...living below his own level." — C. G. Jung

More dangerously, however, you don't realise that there is a shadow at all; you don't acknowledge it, and this is what makes it grow stronger. Don't get me wrong, it's not easy at all but it is your responsibility. All of us have shadows; even some angels have fallen because their shadows prevailed.

Even if you know you are a person of the Light, you must acknowledge your shadow. You must dive into the Deep and meet your own shadow. Only in this way, later on, will you be able to notice the instances in which it manifests in your behaviour in the outer world. If unattended, your shadow interferes with your relationships and choices. The shadow talks and acts for you and instead of you.

The great Carl Gustav Jung observed and analysed the concept of the shadow in an unprecedented and ingenious way. He let his intuition flow through his awe-inspiring amount of research and writing. Jung confirmed that the shadow is difficult to spot and to work with but is nevertheless an essential part of our nature. It is what makes us one unseparated whole.

Only by acknowledging it and learning how to operate with our shadow self (he calls this "shadow work") are we able to learn from our mistakes, and become better, unconflicted individuals. After years of introspection and profound self-reflection, Jung acknowledged his own shadow. He concludes: "How can I be substantial if I do not cast a shadow? I must have a dark side also if I am to be whole."

Acknowledging it doesn't mean that you must accept it for what it is. Understanding and knowing it better is your portal to self-awareness and wisdom. It is your shortcut to knowing your strengths and weaknesses. Casting a shadow behind you is a positive thing. It means that there truly is a light source above you, which casts light directly onto you. At this stage, it is not a matter of "doing" but rather a matter of "knowing". Awakening to this truth, however, causes you a lot of energy and is rarely simple even for the oldest souls who have come on this earth with encoded truths.

"The shadow is a moral problem that challenges the whole ego-personality," Jung writes, "for no one can become conscious of the shadow without considerable moral effort. To become conscious of it involves recognising the dark aspects of the personality as present and real. This act is the essential condition for any kind of self-knowledge. One does not become enlightened by imagining figures of light, but by making the darkness conscious."

AND DO SHADOW WORK

But how does one get around to doing it? You begin with simple steps; otherwise, you might lose yourself. You begin with simple self-reflection. It's like getting to know a new friend whom you just met. It's just like the two boys in my old writing who have just had their spontaneous and fateful encounter. Ask yourself the questions that you would use to get to know the real self of this new person.

What makes you happy? What makes you sad? What is your first memory at all? How about your first memory of guilt? Of anger? Of shame? Of fear? What triggers you? What has traumatised you? What do you dislike in yourself and others?

Think about all of these for a bit. Take your time.

When you carefully reflect on the questions, the answers will intuitively emerge from your unconscious mind. You will spot patterns. The things that you feel guilty or ashamed of, or angry about, are your insecurities. These are the things you are ready to put walls for, or openly attack people for — in order to preserve or hide them. You are ashamed to even think about those insecurities. Maybe sometimes you "project" them onto others in a blind attempt for no one to see that you are the one hiding them. Other times you pile everything inside and the bad feeling of guilt or anger lingers over the years like an untreated wound, directly bleeding onto your confidence and self-respect.

Whether it is justified or not, guilt is part of your shadow. And you have to acknowledge it.

What do you really and deeply feel guilty of? Who put that guilt onto you? Was it you or someone else? Was it a parent or another family member? Was it a friend? Or a lover? Reflect on that. Don't be afraid to mentally travel back to the moment in which that feeling emerged.

But before you let it take over you completely, remember: it is just that — a feeling — nothing more. It doesn't even begin to define who you really are. Don't ever forget that you are a complex and divinely designed mechanism — and one single feeling is just an addition that should not be able to interfere with your solid framework. That is, if you have a strong connection with the Source; and you enrich it diligently. You must always remember that you are a divine creation and God has a plan for you. If you have faith in that, believe me, you have already made the first step of letting go of this unnecessary fragment. You are never alone in your growth, never.

Guilt has another side too. If someone has made you feel guilty in the past and this has lingered inside you, you might consciously or subconsciously start blaming them for the pain that they have caused you. Again, this depends entirely on you as well. This is why realising your shadow is so important — you begin to make better choices, like the choice to forgive. Guilt could turn into something ugly. It could become your reason for attacking others in blind anger, losing yourself in the battle.

Guilt, especially if conscious, could also be your reason to stay in the "victim" mode. Thus, every criticism, even a friendly and constructive one, takes the shape of a sharp weapon pointed at you. That is because you take it through the prism of your insecurities, your shadow. The shadow is not sound and is never a voice of wisdom; if you listen to it often, it inevitably leads you to wrong choices and inadequate behaviours.

And then one fateful morning you wake up and you realise that you don't like yourself anymore...But it is really those dark neglected insecurities that you don't like.

***

I've had my own fair share of guilt and insecurity work. I want to share my story with you so that you can learn from my mistakes. Perhaps, it will remind you of someone else with a similar experience, or it will even bring you back to your own memories.

You see, a big part of my crisis in my teenage years, if not the biggest, was the guilt with which I was unintentionally loaded from my parents. I grew up in a small Bulgarian town and was the only child. My parents didn't have brothers or sisters either. I was the continuation of my poor conservative family, the next of kin, the sole youngest member of the next generation — and a lot was expected from me. I felt as if all eyes were on me, and I had no option of making a mistake.

On the one hand, I didn't mind it that much; in fact, I enjoyed studying and being always at the top of my class, just because. I loved playing with ideas and learning new things, and I appreciated the personal space that was given to me. I loved arts and writing, I loved sciences and even maths. I did it for myself, but the whole family was proud of me. It was another part that was bugging me, though — their emotional instability.

You see, my parents are amazing people - with unique qualities, talents and genes. But they were rather impulsive and irritable when I was growing up; they openly expressed anger and guilt tripping to one another almost on a daily basis. They would fight a lot, throw objects to the walls, and resort to drama. They would shout as much as their vocal cords allowed. They rarely fought physically, but there were such occasions. Both were hurting inside too much. There was alcohol involved at times, too. Somehow, I would often find myself in the midst of the crossfire because they had the tendency to involve me in their adult conflicts. They would make me choose sides or use me as bait so that the other side would see that they have been wrong.

On top of that, all my grandparents and great grandparents (most of them were alive and well when I was a small child) had their own problems and fights. Even though they were obviously not the greatest role models, they did have their opinions about my parents, and were not short on words in expressing them. Gossiping with me and complaining about the wrongdoings of my mother or father pained me. I felt I wasn't doing enough to make the things between my parents and grandparents better. Moreover, I would always come up with reasons why I was to blame for all the wars and separation between the whole family, this lack of balance and purity. I needed to achieve this balance on my own, and I couldn't.

I was four years old when my mother first told me that she was staying with my father only because of me, so that I don't grow up in a broken home with a single mother. I remember I told her back then that if it was better for them to be away from each other, I would understand; I just wanted them to be happy.

She would never leave him, though, she would only talk. But she would unintentionally put the blame on me that she was with a man she was not happy with. For her, it wasn't blame and she didn't realise she was hurting me by saying this. It was her false justification not to do shadow work when it was needed. And that is okay; there is time and place for everything.

Even after all those years, and after a lot of good and bad things have happened to both my parents, they are still together. Only now they have reached some peace, or at least they have concluded a truce to their war. They couldn't acknowledge their shadows the way I wanted them to; the way I knew was right.

It was only later that I found out that there is no "right" way to do that; maybe they did it in their own way. In fact, it is a highly individual process, just as discovering God is. The two processes are connected anyway.

Coming to think of it, this was not a failed mission. At the end everything turned out to be exactly how it should be. Everyone makes their own choices. My own mission here was not to teach them about the lights and the shadows. A child cannot and should not be the wise teacher in the family; it is just an unmanageable burden. My mission here was to rather realise and let go of the burden with which they had unknowingly loaded me, and to forgive them completely. The truth is that by attempting to teach them I gradually became my own advisor and wise teacher.

Every negative aspect makes absolute sense and becomes positive, if you look at it from the perspective of the greater good.

I realise that now, but in my teenage years it was difficult.

The guilt tripping was continuous after my childhood and now it included putting an unintentional blame on me for the financial instability of the whole family. You see, they had to be in a lot of debt in order to move me to one of the most prestigious, private high schools in the country. At fifteen I was obviously going through a crisis and they could see it. However, they were somewhat inept in offering me emotional stability and a safe place to fall when I had my painful insecurities. So their solution was to give more and more money that they didn't have. This resulted in a catastrophe, as my burden of guilt grew exponentially and became something almost unmanageable.

In addition to that, it wasn't by chance that at this time exactly we had a vicious combination of illness, injuries and deaths in the family. It was just too much to take. I felt guilty for all of this, still not facing this feeling and analysing it in a rational and objective way. The shadows had taken over me, and I didn't even realise it. I didn't want to go into the Deep back then and self-reflect, because I was subconsciously already too scared to find what had become of me. And since it pained me a lot, I just kept it settled in there.

I wouldn't take the first step to resolving the problem, which is to acknowledge it exists at all.

This is when at the age of sixteen my rebellious period began. For more than one whole year I became almost unrecognisable. My guilt and insecurities mutated into a dark and angry self-expression. I became cynical, mean and loud; almost nihilistic. I forced myself to like things in pop culture and music which I had found distasteful before. I started listening to extremely hard and dark music, even death metal. I changed my appearance too. I lost weight, I cut my hair and

I would put a lot of dark eye makeup on. Later I put on piercings as well — on my brow (even to this day I have a scar there as a reminder of my inner battles), on my tongue, ears and belly button. A tattoo followed as well, shortly after.

My relationship with my parents reached its all-time low. I would tell them how much I hated them on a weekly, if not on a daily basis. I was inept at seeing any of their numerous good qualities, intentions and actions, and they rather felt like enemies to me. I feel so bad about that now. Back then I didn't even know where all of this hate and anger came from; I was confused and oblivious. And since I could see how my words hurt them, I would unknowingly feed the lurking guilt inside me even more. The worst thing was that they would often fight back and return the mean words to me; I had now become just like their shadow selves.

Understandably, they would put more control over me, which made me rebel even more, as I escaped from home on several occasions. I had no idea where to go or what I was even doing; and was oblivious to the truth that what I wanted to escape from was myself. I was almost intentionally hurting others with my impulsive behaviour.

I started skipping school just for the "fun" of it — the same private school for which my parents worked in sweat and tears to supply with allowance money. The rebellion to my guilt was out of hand, and the word "control" was a distant concept to me. I almost repeated tenth grade. The whole school situation was highly unnatural and novel to me. I had always loved school and studying. But now studying became a burden because I had a hard time concentrating. I had lost my control, motivation, creative flow, my childlike curiosity, as well as my confidence that I could be good at anything.

I became superficial and shallow. I also had the hardest time socialising ever. Relating to that, I am just grateful that in this extremely vulnerable period, I didn't end up in the wrong crowd. That would have ended badly. I suppose the Source had really been watching over me at all times. My friends back then had their issues but were not problematic per se. I would hang out mostly with boys who were gamers and more introverted than anything else. I remember how I was actually the bad influence on them and they followed me blindly. I made them smoke cigarettes and drink alcohol with me so that I wouldn't be alone in my shadows.

Do you get a sense of how this vicious cycle of negativity is also contagious? The unresolved guilt lies deep in your soul and mutates more and more into something ugly with every choice you make to neglect it. This set of choices ultimately makes you a different person. This darkness is often carried out to the next generations and they spread it amongst their circles of friends who in their turn transmit it to their own kids. It never really ends until someone wakes up and ignites the change from within. I wouldn't work on my insecurities related to guilt, and now those insecurities were dangerous to others.

They often say that the opposite of love is fear. I would agree — it is fear of the unknown, fear of change, fear of letting go, fear of what lies beyond. Fear is also the core of other dark culprits such as worry, doubt, anxiety, distress. Fear is deprived of love and also of faith; it is almost like the shadow of love or love in negative photography. And you never see this clearly unless you risk everything and take a single peek into the Deep. However, you must do it through the eyes of a child, with pure curiosity and good intentions.

And revelations inevitably come. The risk is worth it, I promise.

Following the trail of my journey, we come to the point of my own revelations. Fast forward one year and a half, I am seventeen, and I find these old, scattered writings of my nine-year-old self. As I read through them in a quiet moment of introspection, it was not a dramatic event of great enlightenment; far from it. It was a mere grain of truth which was sown into me by none other than my past self. That was all I needed to begin a gradual repair of my character over the upcoming years. I felt as if my soul remembered something. It was vague but I knew it was there. A single sparkle. My first spark of awakening was ignited.

I was intrigued by it, so gradually, I started seeking again. For the first time in years, I began hearing and not just listening. I was curious again. About myself and the world. And more importantly, what exists beyond. I started reading more books and watching documentaries. My creative flow was coming back. I made a few more attempts at writing back then, as they were becoming more and more philosophical. I became nice to people again and strengthened my relationships.

I had a sense of the power of choice. I chose to forgive those who had hurt me, and also ask for forgiveness; I chose to honour my mother and father, and be humble before their love, protection and best intentions. Moreover, I became aware of my parents' great qualities which are simply countless. I almost saw them as different people, in a different light; but all I did was just focus on their own light, rather than darkness.

When you focus on the good in people, you usually bring the best out of them.

I became thankful that I even had my parents in my life

and that I was blessed with a home and a family, unlike many unlucky children. My compassion for them was a continuous act of kindness, and not just a segregated feeling. I was calm, understanding and respectful, which was what they had always deserved, but I had been too blind to see it.

I chose to study hard and improve my grades, and I reached the top of my class again just before graduation. I chose to become my own friend, rather than an enemy. The transition was rather slow, yes, and I had my ups and downs. I would return to my shadows now and then. But at least I was aware of them now, and I knew that I had to let go. That is why this new path felt so bright and welcoming — I was able to see and compare the two paths. The overall transition was so intuitive and graceful that there was no friction; unlike my previous transformation in which I needed to force myself to become someone I am not.

A lot was given to me by the Source in this period.

"For everyone who asks, receives. Everyone who seeks, finds. And to everyone who knocks, the door will be opened." — Matthew 7:8.

Sometimes there were little signs; other times, big revelations or inner realisations.

I remember I was stunned by one particular documentary, which my friends "randomly" found on the internet, and we watched it together — *Zeitgeist*. If you don't know what that is, it is a well-structured exposé of the elite of this world, and their control over normal people like us. The movie reveals all the areas in which we are controlled like oblivious sheep: bank systems, medicine and vaccines, food, pop culture, religion. Of course, everyone should take this movie with a grain of salt because after all it's just that — a movie — a collective of alternative opinions and not everything is correct and unbiased. However, it ignited the second huge flame in my journey of awakening.

I was mesmerised by the concept of people being oblivious to truths which are hidden in plain sight. I became obsessed with conspiracy theories, even made a school presentation about that in my philosophy course. Everyone has gone through this period, right? Exploring what they call "the dark side of YouTube", spending sleepless nights playing a detective and all that. Maybe you remember your own conspiracy rally together with your friends or alone in your room. Exploring the majority of conspiracies is great in my opinion, as long as it doesn't interfere with your relationships and everyday activities.

For me it was very healthy and right on time. I observed the subliminal messages of sexual and aggressive nature in Disney movies for kids and in consumer products, as well as the satanic symbolism in popular music. And I naturally began asking questions about the reason behind all these bizarre elements. "Why?" became my greatest ally. It is such a vital question that you should apply in your life as much as possible, and to everything. "Why?" is a portal to reason, meaning, truth, and growth. It exposes lies and meaningless activities and relationships. It brings you to action.

I didn't have the answers right away. But I kept asking and asking, and reflecting. My inquiries at one point began to take the form of a prayer. It was again a very intuitive and graceful transition. It almost felt organic, like the process of breathing or walking. I was intrigued by the change, so I just followed this new trail I had instinctively discovered. I didn't know whom or what I was asking for answers, but I knew that my soul craved them.

WHY?

Because loads of people choose darkness, that's why.

It is ultimately this. It is the answer to all dark symbolism and happenings in this world. You have to choose your side, and your journey will be dictated by your choice. You will also affect others by your choice; don't forget that. You don't need to know the exact details of how evil operates. But you need to know that it does — and it's very active at that. It interacts with your shadow on an unconscious level.

"For we wrestle not against flesh and blood, but against principalities, against powers, against the rulers of the darkness of this world, against spiritual wickedness in high places." — Ephesians 6:12

You were given free will to decide your path. So when you choose evil, you deviate from God's divine plan for you, and your shadow becomes your ruler. Remember, it is not sound and is never a voice of wisdom. If you trust it, it will inevitably lead you to your own demise. It is very important to be aware of your shadow because that is what makes the difference in your better future choices. You will not be defined as a good person by having no shadow, but by being aware of it and learning how to integrate it.. Naturally, you must choose the light, but you will never know what light is until you have seen your darkness.

Have you noticed that many people who claim loudly to be good Samaritans, have the worst skeletons in their closets?

They push too hard to look innocent and have this almost compulsive need to do good, merely to appear great in the eyes of others. Shadows infiltrate such behaviour very easily. It is again a form of defence mechanism to hide insecurities. On certain occasions this demeanour may also become egotistical and the exact opposite of humble. Those people naturally have a sense of what good and bad is but have done zero shadow work and this still affects their choices and relationships behind closed doors. Finding true light within the soul is not an easy path for anyone, and there are no cheats or shortcuts in this game.

It may be a painful subject, but another example of the level of difficulty is that a lot of priests are secret perverts and child molesters. Don't be hasty to judge. It has nothing to do with religion or faith. It is a human choice to ignore the dark half and the fallen state of humanity. When they ignore that for too long and keep their eyesight only on the light in front, the darkness consumes them from behind. You really need to have a 360 vision within your inner realm to prevent that.

However, as you already know, it is a complex process that takes years of realisations and shadow work. Since priests are living and working exactly in the midst of the constant war between darkness and light, their wrong steps have dire consequences. It is not easy for them at all, and I feel compassion for them. Their souls could get contaminated with fragments of evil at any time. That is why it is vital for them to realise and work on this every day. But when they don't — it is their own choice and not God's plan for them.

Many people tend to justify their disconnection with the Source with the fact that the church is corrupt. They project their own insecurities by putting blame onto an institution.

What does this have to do with your own personal faith and relationship with God? When you think about it, it is very logical that the first thing Evil would target is the institution of Light, and all its members. Evil has done a lot of work over the years to make sure that the Light is suspicious and untrustworthy, that it looks bad, or that it doesn't exist at all.

However, light can only be concealed for so long; it cannot be eradicated. Light is generated, similarly to Nikola Tesla's free energy, within your own faith freely, and within your personal connection with the Source. You can openly transmit it to others as well. Nobody can take that free energy away from you.

"That the gods die from time to time is due to man's sudden discovery that they do not mean anything; that they are made by human hands, useless idols of wood and stone." — C.G. Jung

… but close the door to the outside for a second and look within. Let us take a peek into the Deep together — through the eyes of innocent children. Do you still believe that you cannot find the answers in here? How about the time when you listened to your voice of inspiration and goodness, and this miracle happened? Don't use your human logic on this, because it's irrelevant. Just let the awareness flow through you and let your soul remember things that your mind has forgotten.

"Don't try to comprehend with your mind. Your mind is very limited. Use your intuition." — Madeleine L'Engle, *A Wind in the Door.*

I want you to think about the time when the Voice spoke to you, but you didn't listen. I want you to face your mistake; face your shadow. I want you to ask questions. Why? Why didn't you listen? Who or what did you listen to instead? Was it your ego? Your friends? Your parents? Your influencers on the internet? Or no one… and you were just fooling around without a purpose?

What was the outcome? Did you waste your precious time… or something more? Did you get depressed or frustrated? Did you end up in a meaningless relationship? Or settled for a mediocre job which didn't put your talents and strengths into good use? Did you lose money? Did you end up hurting somebody? Or perhaps you were too proud to forgive someone right before you lost them forever?

Whatever the consequences were, you need to know that you could have done better. It is high time that you admitted it to yourself. It was your choice. But that's OK. That's the beauty of it — we all must make mistakes in order to get to know our shadows better. In this growth you need to be humble, and vulnerable, and open. Now is the time to reflect on it and admit that you were wrong. Only in this way you can grow and develop that 360 vision; unlike the people who proudly chant that they are saints but are unaware of their dark side.

Their experience actually reminds of classic stories like Dr Jekyll and Mr Hyde. The positive main character has a hard time taming his dark half, so he literally loses consciousness when the other negative personality takes over. He has no memory of its wrongdoings. It is a pretty intriguing coincidence that alcoholics and drug addicts, as well as some murderers, hold no memory of their dark crises too. They act on a subconscious mode; "sub" meaning "below the level" of normal awareness and control.

"The conflict between the two dimensions of

consciousness is simply an expression of the polaristic structure of the psyche, which like any other energetic system is dependent on the tension of opposites." — C.G. Jung

I've always marvelled at the symbolism of light and darkness which you can find everywhere. The Yin and Yang symbol says it all. The two opposite energies flow into one another in a constant dance, and together form one perfect circular whole. I've always loved Yin and Yang, as it has been meaningful to me on a subconscious level, and I also like how it looks aesthetically.

There are some major symbols like that which are incorporated within our unconscious, and always give us meanings even if we've never seen them before. Jung calls those archetypes or archetypical symbols. He claims that they can be universally and intrinsically understood by all nations, structures of society, religions and tribes, at any point in history. Rather stunning, isn't it?

Why? Well, at least he explains it with the idea that we all share one hidden collective mind, so to say. It is related to what theosophists refer to "Akashic records" — a cosmic compendium of all human events, thoughts, words, emotions, and intent ever to have occurred in the past, present, or future.

Modern scientists like to call it "hive mind", and they have just begun researching it. It is astonishing. In my opinion, Jung coins the most accurate term for this — he calls it the

Collective Unconscious. I imagine it as a huge stormy realm right above us in the form of flowing energies. We can't perceive it with our physical senses, but we do take information from it with our senses of the soul. This is the realm where good and evil fight, and Yin and Yang do their dance. This is also the realm from which we gain goodness and inspirations from our common Source through rays of light but also pick up hissing whispers from the darkness.

It is also the field in which we influence one another without realising it. You see, we gain knowledge from each other without physically interacting. This is why there have been instances in which a scientist discovers something new after long sleepless nights of research — and on the other side of the earth another random person wakes up with the same ingenious realisation. In the same way, we affect each other in our fear, anger, nihilism, apathy and hate.

"If your hate could be turned into electricity, it would light up the whole world."— Nikola Tesla

It is a complex concept, but essential for you to grasp, because it reveals the importance of your own choices. Your selection affects not only you, but your close circles too, and to a certain extent, they affect the whole humanity. Take into account that not making a choice is also a choice, and there will be consequences for that. By being too absent-minded or negligent, you freely offer your soul to dark influences. This is not a matter of jokes and if you think that this doesn't concern you, you will be surprised by how low you can fall by not caring.

This is the meaning behind phrases like: "the change must start from within" — they are not just some obscure sayings of an old philosopher. The change must really start from within in order for the vicious cycle to be stopped, one soul at a time. Just as a beehive is one collective intelligent organism, the entire humankind is a buzzing system directed by each single member, and all of them as a whole.

This brings me to my next point, which I am sure you have at least heard of...

LAW OF ATTRACTION IS THE FIRST ANSWER

"According to your faith let it be to you." — Matthew 9:29

It has become mainstream pop science at this point. But I will reveal to you another perspective for it, which in my opinion makes it special and explains why it really works.

It works because by following the rules of the law of attraction, what you do in reality is building a strong connection with God. When you choose to be positive, helping, strong and unyielding in achieving your dreams no matter what, you enrich your channel of light. And you affect the whole world with your choice. When you visualise your desires as already achieved, you send off a particular signal to God which resembles a prayer. And if you actually pray for them, there is no stronger signal that you could send off.

The more you enrich this channel of light, the more knowledge is given to you by the Source. This could be in the form of ideas, inspirations, realisations, symbols, or connections. It could be a single sparkle. But if you notice it and put it into good use, it will change your life. It will bring you to action. It will make you make others happy. It will help you achieve your dreams. You might have heard that this means "to attract" something in your life, hence "the law of attraction".

You need to know that this is a half-truth, and not the whole story. It might be just the beginning of your journey of realisation. After all, you are not a magnet, but a human being. The truth is that everything is given to you by the Source because you follow the right path.

However, bear in mind that you will only be gifted in accordance with your own unique design, as well as the mission with which you came on this plane of existence. If something is bad for the growth of your soul, it will not be given to you and you will be thankful later on. Also, a seemingly bad experience could be given to you, but it is actually good in its real nature, looked at from the perspective of the greater good.

According to the same rule, something might be given to you a bit later in life, when it is the right time. You have to grasp the essential difference between wanting and needing. This high-level state of mind requires patience, matured introspection and self-awareness; as well as letting go of ego and materialism.

Everyone has their own missions, and we must apply different tools in order to achieve them. We are all carefully sculpted in a unique way without equivalents. And we can't all have the same experience or same things in our lives. The ultimate number of possessions we can have will come only after we have built our very own connection with the Source; after we have achieved wisdom. Ironically, this is exactly when we don't really want these material possessions anymore because we have discovered that true happiness lies elsewhere.

"Happiness consists not of having, but of being; not of possessing, but of enjoying. It is a warm glow of the heart at peace with itself. A martyr at the stake may have happiness that a king on his throne might envy." — David O. McKay, *Pathways to Happiness*

Even though the mainstream concept of the law of attraction is flawed, it contributes to the awakening of many people. Just as you would imagine, I stumbled upon it again "randomly" just at the right time at nearly eighteen — after I had begun doing shadow work and improved my life a bit. At this period, everything seemed to be going well, and I was taking things step by step.

I had learned a lot of things about the world, and its lies and conspiracies. I had intuitively sensed what was right for me and was putting an effort to achieve it every day. I had forgiven and had been forgiven. But it still felt as if pieces of the puzzle were missing, so I kept asking and asking.

That is when one close friend invited me home because he had "an important documentary to show me". I didn't think that it was anything too special; after all, we used to watch loads of documentaries and movies with my introverted friends back then (not to even mention playing video games). But this film was kind of special. At least for me, at the exact time back then — since it introduced the law of attraction to my life, and I welcomed it with open heart.

As I watched through *The Secret*, I felt so thrilled that there was really something more... a fragment that I had vaguely grasped, but never put into words:

God actually answered back.

The Secret was a curious gem back then. I never read the book anyway, but I didn't need to. I wanted to remain with my old memories of the movie, at this exact moment in my life. Eating popcorn and watching this exciting revelation which may or may not be true, with my friend in our teen years, while life was still somewhat frivolous. We would exchange wide-eyed looks at the most dramatic moments and ask questions we had no answer of.

I felt purified after this movie for some reason. It resonated with me even more than *Zeitgeist*, because it was the right time for it and my soul was ready for the next stage. Still, I immediately sensed this movie had its flaws. However, I was also aware that it was just the beginning. I was thrilled and impatient to upgrade greatly after that, by reading and watching deeper and more serious stuff.

Strangely enough, this wasn't the case with my friend who was the one to show me this beginner's revelation. He obviously wasn't ready for the next step as his soul was still at a lower stage of development. You see, this particular friend had a lot of anger issues. He had his own family problems, self-doubts and personality disruptions; had done zero shadow work which had resulted in temper issues, or passive aggression when he wasn't openly angry.

Just as I had neglected my guilt, he had been extremely reluctant in dealing with his anger; with integrating his dark side. Remember that regardless of the type and shade of your shadow, the same rules apply.

Whether it is guilt or fear, or anger, or aggression, or perversions, or shame, or sadness, or hate, or apathy — the first step is to acknowledge it, then carefully observe it, and tame it with the help of the Great Light.

Unsurprisingly, he was also one of the biggest atheists I ever knew. Still, this documentary obviously moved him in his own way; he must have had his reasons to share it with me. But his soul was just not ready at this point, and he couldn't respond to the message. Who knows, maybe the message was intended for me at that moment — and that's why he found

The Secret in the first place. And then after high school we parted our ways and I never saw him in person again.

When I self-reflect, I often think about that period of my life and the role of my connections back then. Seeing this movie was a stepping-stone in my existence and I would later go back to it over and over again as a reminder of my spiritual journey. *The Secret* seems almost ridiculous to me now as they have excluded the Christian God from the picture and only talk about how the soulless "Universe" will respond to your callings. Ha.

Even if that's the case, it was just a "starter pack" of revelations at that point, and I am glad that it was merely this. Consequently, I became wiser step by step, walking steadily along my path. If I had perceived the big revelations straight away, my mind would have exploded. All steps are important. I know that these initial small revelations were given to me by the Source, through my friends.

The Great Light is so great that it can flow through extreme atheists as well, whether they notice it or not.

Since I kept going back to this very important third major moment of truth, I had the urge to return the piece of knowledge that was given to me. So I found and added this old friend on Facebook several years later. He looked sad in the pictures. It was immediately obvious to me that his life after high school wasn't any easier. I asked if he remembered me. He only replied with "oh, a blast from the past".

And then I asked him straight away, if he remembered the documentary, he had shown me. I explained in detail the messages of *The Secret*, and how they have helped me chase the light and change my life for the better since we last saw each other. I thanked him that he was the messenger of hope back then and told him that now I wanted to return the favour.

It came as a huge surprise that he remembered nothing of it. To my thankfulness he only replied with, "None of this matters now, and I don't believe in any of it." As much as I tried to convince him to take from his own past advice (as I did), he wouldn't listen. As we talked, he didn't seem angry or passive aggressive now, he was rather on the verge of despair, apathy and surrender. He had stumbled upon numerous unresolved obstacles after we last saw each other.

Apparently, he had not done any shadow work in the following years either, and this had led him to yet another void. Moreover, he didn't remember a single thing of the documentary that he had shown to me; the documentary which was the third important step in my ladder to truth, but not his.

I tried hard to enlighten him in my gratitude, but to no avail. Now, he was more unprepared for my messages of hope than ever. But you see, you cannot and should not help everyone. Everyone has their own mission in this life, experience, and pace of learning. Not everyone learns from their past self and past mistakes either. There are many different paths in which you can discover the light and my path did not resemble his, although our roads crossed and there was a reaction.

Some souls learn the truth later in this physical existence, or even at their moments of death. But ultimately, everyone learns it. You just can't force it onto anybody before they are ready. You can be the messenger. But it has to be authentic and natural, not forced. It's just like with this book — I am writing it because self-expression is one of my missions. Hopefully I will also become your very own messenger in an organic, spontaneous way; and just at the right time.

BUT BE WARY OF DARK MESSAGES!

"To pacify your external conflicts, you must wage peace, first and foremost, within yourself." — Vironika Tugaleva, *The Art of Talking to Yourself*

Remember that the Deep is your unconscious realm. While you can find all the inspirations, truths and love in there, you can also stumble upon fragments of evil. Sometimes the dark messages are obvious, but other times they are disguised as light. This is why the right order is to always get to know your shadow first, so that you can detect false light. You truly need to understand why you think and act inadequately or hurtfully in some situations. Don't skip steps. You'd be surprised how fast the shadows overcome you if you think that you're only receiving messages from the light; and that you're always good and right.

"The unconscious is commonly regarded as a sort of encapsulated fragment of our most personal and intimate life — something like what the Bible calls the 'heart' and considers the source of all evil thoughts." — C. G. Jung

Just as the darkest figure in the Bible — Lucifer — is described as the "Light bearer", you could be falsely "enlightened" by deceiving messages. At times the line is very thin, and you have to master your inner perception and that 360 vision in order to distinguish real light from a false one. Remember that the biggest war is waged for your soul; so it's very logical that Evil will try to dominate in the most subtle and dexterous ways. Almost imperceptibly, these subtle ways lead to bigger consequences over time because of the gradual transformation of many deceived humans.

Have you ever wondered why there have been so many wars and conflicts in the world? Have you noticed the underlying tendency to fight for peace, an oxymoron in its nature? If we are at the point where we need to fight for our beliefs and for inner peace, it is already too late. Chaos is present, as the order of peace has been disrupted. Peace is achieved on the inside first, and on a very intimate level with one's own self. Only later is it externalised and visible in the person's actions and choices of battle.

Stop turning every single battle into your own. Sometimes amidst all wars, what you need to become is a lighthouse, not a sword. — Akshay Vasu

The truth is that absolute justice does exist. It comes from the Source exclusively. Knowing this, you should take a breath and relax. Realise that the burden of establishing supreme equality doesn't lie on top of your fragile human shoulders. It is ridiculous to think that any human, or combination of humans, is capable of establishing perfect balance on this physical plane on their own. This has been tried and tested in the past with numerous political and social systems; all of which unsuccessful, because our inner fallen state prevails every time. So why seek absolute justice externally, or even vengeance? It never leads to anything good.

Don't be a warrior before you have become a wise sage. Otherwise, going into battles unprepared will ultimately cost you your soul — the treasure for which the biggest war is waged.

There is one particular dark message disguised as light

which is detrimental to the souls receiving it. Unfortunately, it is so subtly deceptive that a huge majority of people trust that it is actually a bright message of truth. This is the belief that you are perfect — just the way you are. This dark message preaches that you should "love yourself more than anyone and anything else". "Don't let anyone tell you that you are wrong." "The world must change in accordance with your standards, but not you — because you are just perfect." "You must fight for your beliefs so that you can prove to society how worthy and special you are." "You must get and get and get before you give, because you must take care of yourself first."

The distorted concept of "loving thyself" in our times is the root cause of all evil. It leads to egotistical and narcissistic behaviour, and loss of touch with reality. "Loving" yourself more than anything and anyone else leaves you disabled. Half-human. You lose your empathy, tact, communication skills and dare I say, intelligence. It's harder and harder to tell right from wrong too. But still, you prefer to fight for your unstable beliefs in an absurd attempt to push your insecurities deeper and deeper. You willingly cease your spiritual growth and character development, because you repeat to yourself that you are perfect just the way you are. The consequences are stagnation and later on, decay.

Ultimately, you lose your soul. It's actually Evil's most proudly elaborated shortcut to winning you over. The point of extreme egoism, consumerism, indulgences and physical pleasures is just a step away if you go on this path. Upon reaching it, you leave your soul behind unkempt. And that's the easiest and most convenient way for it to be snatched from the shadows.

Remember that when you don't want to make the

conscious choice to be better, you are making another underlying choice — to accept whatever comes your way, and whoever you are turning out to be. And as this false light attacks your spirit in dexterous ways, you unknowingly, but openly, take in the seven deadly sins: pride, greed, lust, envy, gluttony, wrath and sloth.

In that sense, when you "love" yourself more than anything else, you willingly accept the philosophy of hedonism. This philosophy claims that we are only here in this world to experience pleasures, and that's why we constantly seek them in one way or another and fight over them. Whether it is sex or food, or substances, or belongings, or power — pleasure is our drug of choice, and it is what we are living and dying for, according to hedonism.

Upon reading this, if you feel somewhat repelled or offended, your intuition works just fine and you should be happy about it.

This theory is disgusting and yet another product of lies. Are we really just some creatures roaming around in search of satisfaction, stealing pleasures from one another and hiding in the shadows?

This is definitely one part of us. This is our dark side that we should learn to manage and get to know better. This is our Mr Hyde. But Evil will try to make you believe that there is nothing more to you; and you might as well make the best of it — at least to have some fun while you are here. "You only truly have the present moment, so enjoy it to the fullest." It is indeed all fun and games, until your soul stagnates, and you begin to hate yourself and others, and don't have the slightest clue why.

Don't ever forget that you were designed and sent here.

You didn't emerge from nothing. You have a mission and a purpose. You are not here just to have fun, so don't take it light-heartedly. You were gifted with this great Voice, your intuition, to guide you in your very own purpose; to operate as an inner compass pointing right and wrong. Cherish it and be thankful for it. Be aware that there are things greater than you and be humble; love the Source more than your own self; and be relieved from that. Show love and compassion to people; love thy neighbour as thyself.

The Truth will set you free.

Get to know more about yourself and this Voice. Don't be afraid to meet your shadow; but strive to become a better person. Your soul is like an unfinished sculpture and you are the artist — work on it constantly. You can never be perfect on this physical plane, but you can always be better. It doesn't have to be a burden, although it is indeed hard work. Accept it as a journey of a lifetime; a dangerous expedition with a set of challenges but with a trophy at the end — because that is what it is.

If you choose this path, in time you will see how everything else slowly becomes a background noise. No distractions from the shadows can lead you astray from your bright path to achieving your purpose. Be wary of dark messages. But also know that you are naturally more receptive to light — and pure light truly feels different from a false one.

"Your visions will become clear only when you can look into your own heart. Who looks outside, dreams; who looks inside, awakes." — C.G. Jung

You are indeed designed to explore and express your truths, but in the right way and at the right time. Rushing it will just make things complicated. After you have become entirely self-aware, you won't have the need to fight or go into battles to prove your point. People will believe you and come to you on their own. You will love and respect yourself in the TRUE way, appreciating your growth and all the help that was gifted to you by the Source. You will emanate light, and the truth will flow through your voice on its own. To become a wise sage first is not simple, but it is the correct order of things.

SHARING YOUR VISIONS IS THE SECOND ANSWER

All of these truths so far are even more powerful when shared with kindred spirits. It is the pure reason why I am sharing my personal journey with you in vulnerability and humility. It is also the reason why in my early twenties, I underwent yet another transformation which was complex but absolutely essential to my fate now. The period of this transition feels so surreal now, almost as if I was in a dream state. But the outcome, after the veil lifted, was even more unbelievable...

You see, after graduating high school and entering university, I had a "tiny" break from all that deep stuff. I became engaged in my daily routine again — I had a lot to study and spend energy on, so I just left everything else "on hold". My studies in linguistics were a huge part of my growth because they included a lot of critical thinking, writing and creative expression. However, I still felt I was suppressing a need for something more.

In addition to my almost full-time university responsibilities, I would take part-time jobs to support my study expenses. I would also do sports intensively. I became much more sociable, as I would go out on weekends and even during the week. That whole mixture of activities had left me with practically no spare time for any major self-reflecting process.

I didn't have significant inner conflicts back then; I had

already been on the bright path for some time. But I didn't make any huge leaps forward either. I was calm and confident, and I was yet again at the top of my class. Everything was going well for me, and my motivation level was at its peak. I was already within more intelligent and interesting circles of friends than before... but I still had that gnawing feeling that I was missing something big; and it was the key to taking the next step.

It took me some time to realise that I just didn't have the right people to share that vivid inner world of mine with. That's what I was missing. To this day, it has been one of the biggest parts of the puzzle. Knowing the truth is not enough. You need to bring yourself to action. You have to sense and attract the right souls to you — so that you can share that warm feeling of mutual understanding, which is beyond any words. Finding your kindred spirits will contribute to your mutual growth and happiness and will make your overall quality of life better.

I didn't have these souls anywhere near me back then; so naturally I began wondering if there was something wrong with me instead. I tried to suppress this deep side of me in order to blend in. I would only read and watch deep stuff on my own and would hardly ever share my true interests openly — even though they fascinated me and were pretty much all that I thought about. I tried to share my beliefs on a couple of occasions, but they were met with ridicule, lack of interest or coldblooded reasoning of materialistic scientific theories.

It wasn't a big deal, at least not at the beginning. I have a fun side too, so having fun with my friends was a delight. If we did have an intellectual conversation, it would be about the knowledge of the world, new discoveries, and from time to time — conspiracies. That was good enough for me for a while. I cherished those rare moments which unleashed my trail of thoughts and introspection, even for a few minutes. However, I didn't get to express my inner truths and connect with somebody with the same worldview as mine, on a deeper level. I still appreciated other points of view and learned from them.

My feeling of being different didn't go away as I thought. It made me feel a bit sad to see everyone else light-spirited and fitting in so well, and me as always making everything complicated and deeper than it has to be. While I was liked and accepted by all cliques now, because of my kindness and confidence, I still hadn't found my own pack. And time was passing by, as were people. I had already met a lot of different people even though I was just in my early twenties, because I had lived in three different cities already.

I started questioning again. Was there really such a thing as my pack? At this point, I truly doubted that I would ever experience this feeling I was longing for so deeply. Connection. I was already growing tired of making all other people happy, as much as I enjoyed it. I would spend all my time with them making them laugh and feel good about themselves, as I would go home again and again with drained energy and a hungry soul.

I was in an unsuited long-term relationship back then, which didn't help either. He was a very good guy and treated me really well. But he was just deprived of this deep underlying world of colours, symbols, visions and realisations, which had always been my distinguishable trait. Or maybe I had this additional unnecessary fragment which was a bug in the system? I was still questioning this back then. In any case,

I knew that we were not made for each other. At least we didn't fight, and I made myself believe that this was the definition of a fitting relationship.

My intuition had been telling me to let go, right from the beginning. But I stayed. And we adapted to one another's routines so quickly that I forgot what it was all about. My intuition was also telling me that I was right to think, read, and talk about God and his plan for us. But my mind was telling me to chill and adapt to my boyfriend and the other people around me — because they were good enough.

Good enough. What a dangerous category. First of all, the same person could be heavenly for someone else, but just not for me. And the same goes for me and someone else. So my categorisation for him wasn't fair. However, I was not fair to either of us in those several years of relationship. If I had already realised that our relationship was merely good enough, why did I waste his time too?

The answer is that I was honestly losing hope that I would assemble my pack or meet my real soulmate ever. My boyfriend looked happy with me too, at least when I wasn't being weird with my questioning of the universal truth and all that. After all, I was trying hard to like his hobbies and interests, even though they felt somewhat meaningless and time wasting for me, which bugged me a lot. However, I was slowly getting used to the idea of settling down for something secure which was already here and now, and for which I didn't have to seek relentlessly. I felt tired.

Besides, we had already come to the point where it seemed impossible to break up. University years were passing too quickly, and we had been living together for the most part. Our families knew each other; we happened to live almost on the same street in our small home town. We had the same circles of friends and everyone categorised us as an inseparable whole, especially when we were invited to weddings and such.

The clock ticked and I had to do something. I felt trapped but had procrastinated making a decision for too long already. I tried to find the time to self-reflect and pray at this moment because it had now become urgent and inevitable. I prayed and questioned everything, seeking answers and listening closely to the Voice once again.

I remember I would go pointlessly around the beautiful university city I was living in — Veliko Tarnovo — with the public transport. I would put my acoustic guitar music on, as I would enjoy the sunset and the scenery, as well as the beautiful ruins of the medieval part of the city. As I moved around in the city bus, I would think, and think, and think. I got to know myself better during these introspecting moments, even though on the surface they seemed as nothing special.

I would fantasise about different paths from the one I was heading on, and they excited me. I would imagine meeting new people who were very similar to me, and the thrilling feeling of discovering our similarities. I would also fantasise how I would meet my soulmate in thousands of different scenarios, each more romantic and purer than the last one.

I would also wish for all that and pray for it, because it felt right. Besides, at this point I knew that everything was still in my head. More importantly, however, I had the right answer now. I had listened to the Voice and had allowed my imagination to unfold in quiet moments of self-reflection.

My intuition didn't fail me. I had a breakthrough idea which came more in the form of a passionate feeling in my upper abdominal area. I suddenly wanted to travel. I wanted to explore. I wanted to meet new people from other countries as well. And if this was even possible — to finally find my pack.

I wanted to give hope a last chance before settling down. It was a scary decision, because it meant a route change in my relationships, emotions, settings, activities and overall mindset. It was a damn big risk. But I knew that it was just the right thing to do, because it resonated with me completely on the inside.

I knew that I would change once again, and for the better — I would become stronger, more adaptive and flexible; I would change my focus and refresh my vision in this way. I would exchange the melancholy and difficulty of my breakup with starting anew, and going away for a while. The breakup was indeed heart-breaking even though it was the right thing for both of us, but it healed in time; more slowly than I expected, however.

My ex-boyfriend would later find just the right girl for him. They are now happier than ever, already married, and they have a baby. Talking about the greater good...

In the course of three years, I would travel around Europe. I would come back to Bulgaria for a while, and then I would hit the road again. I visited Switzerland, Austria, Germany, the Netherlands, Belgium, France, Czech Republic, Slovakia, Slovenia, and the whole United Kingdom. It wasn't just a meaningless wandering — I always found a way to organise a very specific journey to each of those countries, with specific missions or target qualifications.

The Source gave me abundance with cheap choices of trips and residence, and reason behind each route. That seemed impossible to everyone. People would always ask me how the hell I was doing it. I would get this question about many things from then on, not just travelling.

My journey would not even stop there, and I would later on travel to the Scandinavian lands too, but after the initial three-year period I sensed that it was time for me to go back home, at least for a while. Those trips truly changed my life and were a big part of my key transition back then to become the bright person I am today. They have all been so saturated, creative, challenging and unique that I just have to write a whole different book just about them. But the main point is I did become stronger while I was abroad. On the majority of my trips I was completely alone, and I had to rely merely on my own intuition, adaptability and resourcefulness to survive, stay safe and reach my goals.

The Voice in me became inhumanly powerful during my travels.

In my self-reflecting moments, looking out the window of the plane or train, I physically felt my connection with God getting stronger, in real time. He had been showing me so much from both the beauty and the challenges of this world, and there was so much more I was ready to take on. I was so thankful and full of appreciation that I literally wanted to cry. The Source had gifted me with the right amount of time and the right mindset to self-reflect, explore, and assess my life up until now. He had allowed me to recharge completely.

Most importantly, he helped me assemble my own small pack of kindred spirits. This came to my life as more of a relief than a surprise. My previous doubts were shattered. Now I knew that there were others like me: a different breed of friends, in whose company I felt understood and welcomed in sharing my beliefs. They weren't that many, but enough to share unforgettable moments with. We knew that since each of us was from a different country, our paths would separate soon. But this might have even made it more special — because we weren't afraid to open our hearts right from the beginning and share our visions in warm understanding.

This is why I am so proud to have listened to the Voice, which had resonated with my wishes completely. I received help on every step of the way too, which was yet another proof of how closely guarded I was from the Source. I will never forget that mighty feeling of being in the right place, at the right time, doing the right thing. You can have this as well, if you just listen closely...

***

When I returned after this three-year period of going back and forth, everything had changed. I had changed. My family had major problems again. But this time, I was the unyielding force which was there to keep them safe and sane. I helped them with everything humanly possible, and slowly but surely, they got back on their feet after the crisis. I was also affected by this crisis; after all I am part of the family too. But I chose to be tough, so that I could be the safe lighthouse amidst the wars.

During this period, I had a hard time believing I was that same inadequate, negative and insecure girl from high school. She felt like someone I distantly knew, but nothing compared to my real character or potential. I was now the sensitive but powerful leader of the family, who had let go of all childhood traumas and teenage angst. I was a responsible, stable and compassionate adult. I felt God's force guiding me so strongly that I knew at this point nothing and no one could make me doubt it anymore.

I also felt that I had begun emanating a specific light from within towards the others, and this reflected in the way they responded. I was slowly beginning to change people for the better, only with my voice and my pure energy. My physical voice had also gotten stronger and more expressive.

Around that same time one particular quote by a famous Bulgarian journalist made a huge impression on me. He had always been great at exposing the truth about vibrations, law of attraction, hidden secrets and lost knowledge — Stoycho Kerev. He said something I would never forget: "A person's energy flows through the gaze and through the voice." It really must be so, as you can easily pick up the charge in the sound vibrations of the person's voice. And everyone knows how some people have that special sparkle in their eyes; and how the eyes are indeed the windows to the soul.

My increased frequency started drawing new people to me, as they were attracted by it. They didn't really understand what my power really was, so they would categorise it as "being positive", "being lucky" or just "being beautiful". They would compliment me, on how differently they saw me from the average person. However, they would ascribe all of that to my outlined intelligence and mere positivity. I didn't even see myself as intelligent or as that positive; but I knew that my strength came from a higher power, and from a set of choices that I had made in the distant and recent past.

When I attempted to explain this truth, they would take it in ridicule and disbelief — as if I was just a pretty girl and everything was handed down to me. There was nothing more to it. I was just lucky, and everything must have been easy for me. They knew nothing about me, but they were confident in their guess that I had everything, and could have everyone, if I wanted to. So in a way, they ignored their own intuition about what was different about me, when I directly answered their question. Unfortunately, this is how tiny deception works. It makes you ignore the real light sometimes, although it is right in front of you.

I was almost twenty-four back then. I had moved back to my university town Veliko Tarnovo, alone. Started a full-time office job and signed up for my first Masters studies remotely — linguistics again (later I would study psychology as well). My job then was difficult as it required extreme organisation and communication skills. Even though I was a junior, nobody helped me with anything in the office. This was yet another challenge that was given to me, so that I could overcome it in the correct way. Remember that none of the people you meet in your life appear by chance. They are either there to teach you how to do something, how not to do something, or to be taught by you; or all at once.

In that office I found myself in a circle of unfriendly women. Very strange combination of characters; it became apparent to me right from the beginning how they would transfer negative energy to one another without noticing. It was curious to me rather than anything else. Since I had analysed the situation, I was ready to overcome the challenge. I promised myself to stay strong and positive no matter what; and I reminded myself not to get involved in their battles, because they were not mine. And at the end of the day, it was just a job and I had no intention of making it my career or retiring there.

My colleagues would gossip, stress each other out and blame each other for making mistakes, rather than helping or training one another how to do things right. They would resort to complaining and passive aggression all the time, because it was the easiest way to go. As I was the new girl and youngest member of the team, at one point I became their scapegoat; the vessel for negative energy, so that they could finally unite even in their negativity.

They were not hesitant to backstab me and sell me out to the "big boss", who would proceed with scolding and shouting, penalties, salary deductions, etc. However, I was already strong enough to act cold-bloodedly in this toxic environment, and not take anything personally, as I would actually learn from my mistakes, as well as all others'.

Seeing me this calm, gathered, and uninvolved in the battles made them go crazy. They tried to guilt trip me that since I wouldn't get emotionally involved, it meant that I didn't care about my job. On the contrary, the essence of the job was actually pretty intriguing to me. When I got a hold of it on my own, since there was no one there to train me, I was actually doing a pretty decent job and enjoyed the majority of my work.

You see, it is your own choice to make everything unnecessary a background noise. You must only learn how to introspect, analyse, and not get involved in other people's battles in your way to achieving your present goals. It was obvious to me how unhappy those people were. But you can't help everyone. I had learned my lesson — so I didn't even try.

I would go to the university from time to time just for catch up lectures, since the Master's programme was predominantly remote. I didn't even want to make any friends. I just wanted to enjoy my lessons and forget about work for a while. It turned out that my fellow students were pretty cool, though, so I didn't mind hanging out with yet another fun-loving group of friends. Surely, they weren't deep at all, but I had already gotten used to that at this point. They were just fun to be around, and we clicked quite fast, so I appreciated the lightness of their company a lot.

There was one particular guy from the group who was quite fond of me. I saw him as a friend, and I didn't share his feelings. But I thought that I might use this situation to share some light with him, because after all that was what drew him to me in the first place. He would say that he was becoming a better person around me for some reason. He was quite the romantic and poetic type, so he would often say that he saw me as "a rare shining star", and that my laughter was healing. I was deeply moved and humbled by that, and it gave me hope that I could help him find the light and the healing power within himself. Paradoxically, though, he was an extreme atheist and didn't "believe" in energies at all, although he apparently felt them in me.

I had become so confident in my knowledge back then that I didn't mind having a friendly dispute with him about the truth of our creation and missions in this world. He would argue back that everything was pointless, and that he didn't come from God but from his mother and father. I felt disappointed with how that was possible — smart people could be deceived so easily. Especially those who only trust science. Science answers a lot of questions but is limited, as is human mind and logic.

We have only one tiny blurry window to the real world, to our real home, and to the truth, and this is our vague additional sense called intuition. The vision gets clearer if you gaze through that window often, but if you turn your glance away from it, the vision becomes obscure in time.

I couldn't contribute to the way he felt about the world and himself. I couldn't resonate with his poetic side either. I guess I was just a disappointment to him because I was an un-actualised crush. This is why I know now that I wasn't in the right position at all to try and teach him, even though he appeared ready. It may even be my fault if he never peeked from the window of intuition again, in the search for truth.

Since I was the messenger of light, and at the same time I didn't say yes to his requests, he felt repelled by the messages and warded them off before giving them a chance to resonate with him. He felt angry and frustrated that I was so deep into my knowledge of a higher power. He was also smart and insightful enough to see that he wasn't a good match for me in that important aspect.

Our paths separated soon after, but my encounter with him had made me realise something essential. From then on, I couldn't allow myself to be with somebody who didn't share my knowledge and mindset. I couldn't be with somebody who hadn't known himself completely and hadn't ventured into the world of imagination and possibilities. I couldn't be with someone who hadn't unlocked his intuition, creativity, and knowledge of the Source. I couldn't be with someone other than my kindred spirit, my mirror self.

I was aware that it appeared ludicrous and impossible, and there were thousands of reasons why that wouldn't happen. But I had just one single powerful reason to believe that it would actually happen — God.

My intuition confirmed that it was the right way to go. At this point, it was either everything at once or nothing at all. I made a promise to myself that I would never waste my time or anybody else's time again in meaningless relationships. This included any relationship that wasn't with the One. At almost twenty-four years of age, I was ready for something more. For the full package.

I was ready for my soulmate.

FINDING YOUR SOULMATE IS THE KEY TO EVERYTHING ELSE

"… and when one of them meets the other half, the actual half of himself, the pair are lost in an amazement of love and friendship and intimacy and one will not be out of the other's sight, as I may say, even for a moment…" — Plato

If you think that soulmates only exist in fictional novels and romantic comedy films, you are wrong. Let's assume you are a strong believer now, and you trust God and his plan for you. Do you think he would make you walk alone in this? Nothing could make Him happier than to see you happy with your other half. After you have become ready, there is no point in leaving you on your own anymore.

But what does ready mean? Before meeting your half, of course, you need to become one unseparated whole. It's quite a counterintuitive metaphor, I know. But I am sure you understand the meaning of that. Being ready means to be extremely aware of your full self — both your lights and your shadows. Jung calls this complex but liberating process individuation.

"Man becomes whole, integrated, calm, fertile, and happy when (and only when) the process of individuation is complete, when the conscious and the unconscious have learned to live at peace and to complement one another." — C.G. Jung

Additionally, you must know your weaknesses and

strengths in a relationship, so that you are aware of how much you give and how much you take. You must be aware of your triggers, projections, and ego displays. More importantly, you must be extremely sensitive to your ideals and what really makes you the happiest person in the world. Ask yourself questions and turn it into an internal dialogue. What really makes you "You"? What kind of partner would fit in well with this uniqueness? Where can you find them? Where can you not find them?

Remember, you must feel really comfortable within your own company before you go out looking for the One. You need to make a promise to yourself and your future half that you will become a better person every day. You must truly know what you are getting into, and you have to believe that the next person that comes as a romantic interest will indeed be your soulmate, and nothing less. You have to sense the qualities of this person and how they make you feel, before you have met them. Don't be afraid or ashamed to fantasise and visualise different scenarios as I did.

"When deep down in the core of your being you believe that your soulmate exists, there is no limit to the ways he or she can enter your life." — Arielle Ford

Try to make out what that person looks like, sounds like, feels like. What they do for a living, and what their favourite hobbies are. Imagine how perfectly synchronised you are in your beliefs and ideas, and how you complement each other's knowledge perfectly like two connecting puzzle pieces. Imagine the two of you in different scenarios and sceneries, accompanied only by a warm excitement and a pure mutual understanding.

Have a sense of how blissful and strong you will become

together with such a person who shares your visions, and who is always there for you. Imagine how much you can grow together. Feel the harmony of living with this person; of the sweet little gestures that put happy tears in your eyes. Feel the beauty of being vulnerable and sincere with someone who will also be like this for you. Be relieved that your soul will be hungry no more, as he or she will be just as intrigued by your things as you are. Think about the humour you will share, and the endless inside jokes you will have just between yourselves. Imagine the respect you will have for one another.

Most importantly, have a sense of the choice you will make to have a life with this exact person, as opposed to choosing anyone else from the other seven and a half billion people on the planet. Imagine choosing no one but your mirror, in a way.

"The soulmate is what we aspire to and like to understand about our self, is what we deem to be perfection, purity, and endless love." — Sorin Cerin

When you visualise and pray for that in pure thought and longing, you will emanate very special and strong signals. Your person might even pick up the signals from miles away, from the collective unconscious network. It won't be on a conscious level, but they will definitely be drawn to you unconsciously at the right time. Or the other way around — you could be the one drawn to them first!

In any case, the main rule here is for both of you to be ready and seek the other person internally. If one or both of you aren't ready, your paths will disconnect, and you might never meet each other. Or you might still meet but it wouldn't be the right time or place, because you are still not one full whole with yourself. And although you will inevitably feel a strong unexplained connection, you just won't feel capable of handling this powerful relationship at that exact moment.

This is why so many people don't "believe" in soulmates. Or they call soulmates merely the life partners with whom you make consensus for better mutual understanding. Come on now, this is not a business deal or a contract. This is a unique connection of the souls, beyond any agreements or even words. For me, such poor definitions honestly represent a mere pat on the back for people who weren't ready to meet their soulmates, and they never did. So they just discourage everyone else that the term doesn't exist at all, or that it means something else.

Soulmate means exactly what it sounds like — a real twin of your soul; your reflection; your kindred spirit; your lover, and your best friend. And I assure you, it is something very real and the majority of people have it. It depends on you, and you entirely, how quickly you will have your soulmate in your life, or if you will meet them at all.

Some people never meet their shadows in the first place, so they are oblivious to the ways they repel their partners. Those people will never find their soulmates. Others are constantly in the victim mode, so they are very far away from being one full whole with themselves. If they don't analyse and fix themselves from within, they will never attract the right respectful partner they deserve.

"Before you find your soulmate, you must first discover your soul." — Charles F. Glassman, *Brain Drain — The Breakthrough That Will Change Your Life*

KEEP YOUR FOCUS ON THE 8TH PATH!

Meeting your soulmate requires a considerable amount of self-purification beforehand. This is very logical as well. How could you meet your mirror self if you are not in your pure form? If you are not your real self? If you are wearing a mask, this other person will be wearing one too, and they won't be your true soulmate. You must be good and have pure intentions and self-expression, in your "waiting room" for the One. You must tame down your ego and be humble. I am sure you are seeing the patterns already — how everything good begins from within, from self-awareness and self-work.

I will acquaint you with the seven paths of going into a relationship without working on the self, first, and without reflecting on one's intrinsic lights and shadows. Think about the ultimate outcome in each of the paths. Remember your own experiences, or the experiences of people you know:

1st Path: You enter into a relationship out of boredom, so you get bored with the relationship quite quickly too. You don't do anything meaningful with your partner and your whole mindset revolves around killing some time with them here and there. Your relationship has no roots, and you don't know much about your partner; but you don't even want to know, because you have already deemed them "boring". So eventually you break up with them, or they break up with you — and you are left in your boring, pointless everyday routine again.

2nd Path: You get together with someone just for superficial reasons — ego, status, money, physical looks, exclusively for sex, social opinions, etc. The relationship is meaningless, and very soon core problems emerge. It is highly unlikely that the people who enter such relationships would pick up this book at all; but if you are one of them and you are reading this, please make sure to reassess your whole value system — not just your relationship preferences.

3rd Path: You get together with someone out of loneliness, although it is very obvious that this is not the person for you. You want to fill a certain empty space in your soul, so you think that being with the first person that came in your way will make things better. However, they are just not a good fit and you give out yourself to them, almost in charity, without receiving much in return. Your soul void grows bigger and it becomes more difficult for you to manage. The relationship ends sooner rather than later, and in more pain than your original state.

4th Path: You decide to go into a relationship out of revenge on somebody with whom you just broke up, or because you want to forget them. However, you are still filled with the emotions, triggers, traumas and shadows of that past relationship. The chances are that instead of getting a better partner, you attract a similar or even a worse partner, who breaks your heart even more brutally. And now you make assumptions that all men, or all women, are exactly the same.

5th Path: You are truly looking for the One or at least you think you are, but you are just not ready, because you didn't get to know yourself enough first. Naturally, you don't know exactly what you need and what "the One" even means. So you are looking here and there, and you stumble upon someone who kind of looks like the One but you have your doubts. You enter into this relationship anyway and there are two possible paths: you either manage to reach a consensus and establish a long-term partnership (but always wonder at the back of your mind "What if..."); or everything ends badly sooner or later, depending on your temperaments and agreeableness levels.

6th Path: You are not looking for "the One" per se, or you don't believe in that. You are just looking for a successful and serious relationship with a decent man/woman. You find them and everything works out great, but in time you sense that it is not enough. So everything ends up in bitterness. Or worse off, you live your life with this person with whom you are not completely happy and satisfied, and they aren't either. So you waste each other's potentials in meeting the right person at the right time. This could indeed be the most successful relationship after the perfect one with your real soulmate; however, if you are an idealist like me, you shouldn't settle for anything less than ideal.

7th Path: There is an exception. Sometimes "fate" knows its job, so it connects two completely unfitting souls spontaneously, who create together either something beautiful or something disastrous. Throughout history, we have seen many great philosophers, psychologists, writers, and inventors who have grown up in broken or unhappy homes, and yet they have become pillars in society with their special missions, overcoming their traumas in a beautiful way. But then again, a lot of diagnosed psychopaths came out of such unfitting parent relationships too. So are you willing to take the risk? And are you willing to put that inevitable burden on your children? Even if it doesn't seem like a big burden to you now, it multiplies with every next generation. And if they don't "wake up" and stop the vicious cycle of unfitting relationships, it will continue on and on, creating a bigger unconscious burden on a higher scale every time.

There is another way, and you already know it. An 8th path which is universally right. You can only feel it intuitively, as it happens with everything true in this world. It is the most exciting way to enter a relationship too; a journey of two kindred souls.

Keep your focus on the 8th path.

The 8th path leads to positive transformations and adventures and dictates your fate and the one of your future generations. The 8th path means doing it all right and starting a relationship with your real soulmate. Focus on the 8th path and don't be afraid to set out for it.

After all, selecting the right person to spend your life with is indeed your ultimate choice. So don't take it lightly. On that single choice depend the lives of your future generations, their genes and characters, as well as their behaviours and their own relationships in time. They don't have a saying in your selection at this moment, so think about them too when making it. How correct you were in your decision will be sensed in the overall atmosphere of the whole family. Both nature and nurture are included in this ultimate choice.

Don't be egotistical; and choose wisely. Don't forget that your partner will be making the ultimate choice with you too, so take this role responsibly and lovingly. Manage your shadow first and be pure in approaching your soulmate. If everything up to this point is done correctly, the encounter itself, as well as what follows after, should be more magical than any fairy tale or fiction novel that you have read in your whole life.

"A soulmate is someone who has locks that fit our keys, and keys to fit our locks. When we feel safe enough to open the locks, our truest selves step out and we can be completely and honestly who we are; we can be loved for who we are and not for who we are pretending to be. Each unveils the best part of the other. No matter what else goes wrong around us, with that one person, we are safe in our own paradise." — Richard Bach.

SEEK AND YOU SHALL FIND

My seeking after these realisations wasn't too long. In fact, my soulmate came into my life right after my conclusion, and in the most unexpected way.

I was still living in my university town in a rented apartment, still working in the same peculiar office, and almost finishing with my first Master's. I had been living alone for some time now, and even though I felt very comfortable in my own company, I had the strong urge to finally find the One. I made myself busy all the time so that I don't think about it too often; however, the feeling remained. It has always been harder for me to suppress emerging feelings than intrusive thoughts. Usually, the feelings are the expressions of your body-soul-spirit network, and thoughts are the extension of that; however, they are all interconnected.

During one lazy Saturday at home, I downloaded the Tinder app almost as a joke. I didn't think too much of it, and I had heard what they said about the app, i.e., what it was all about. "It never hurts to try," I thought. I was pretty excited to look into the dating pool for the first time in my life. Of course, I never stopped focusing on the potential eighth path, even though it seemed like a distant concept, irrelevant to Tinder.

As I would swipe left and right, no one made a huge impression on me apart from their looks. I remember how I had an internal argument with myself at that time, "What more would you expect? These are just some pictures. You don't know these people and what they are really like in person. So anyone from these guys could be your soulmate for what it's worth!"

Even though that sounded absolutely logical, my intuition was telling me to keep seeking without making compromise. The Voice was my greatest ally again, as I would listen to it for any spontaneous impressions on any of the guys. Not to be forgotten that I had already instinctively worked on the visualisation of my soulmate, and no one so far was matching my internal picture. I knew that was extreme but in my mind it was fair.

Besides, the way they approached me in the chat and the way they responded when I approached them was uninteresting. Either small talk or awkward flirting that didn't resemble my style; from time-to-time jokes, but not my type of jokes. They didn't get my references either. Perhaps I was too harsh, but I knew exactly what I wanted because I had imagined it over and over again. Besides, I knew the cost of getting into an unsuited relationship and wanted to keep my promise to the end no matter what happened — for the other person's sake and for my own sake. So I just swiped hundreds of pictures, as the activity was getting more and more boring.

… until I finally stumbled upon him.

All of his pictures looked so different and colourful; and they stood out from everyone else's. I could see on one of them that he was a musician that participated in the show X-Factor. Another picture with a guitar near a river, and a couple more in nature — one of them was on top of a hill, and he looked exhilarated and inspired from reaching it. And one selfie in a train with the sun shining from outside the window, creating inspiring flares — almost an exact copy of my selfies I had made in trains during my own travels. He had also included one painting which was so surrealistic, symbolic and cool that intuitive interpretations started flooding in me spontaneously about his character and experiences. His last picture must have been from Halloween, as he had the makeup and style of one of my favourite anime characters.

It may sound stupid, but I felt a particular connection just by looking at his pictures. For one thing, they were aesthetically appealing to me and I found myself in them. It was obvious that he was a person of both visual art and music, who loved nature and travelling — and probably the same things in popular culture as me, judging by the anime picture.

More importantly, however, I noticed his gaze; there was something very special about it. His eyes had this peculiar sparkle — a strong flame which made his whole face light up and radiate a confident and pure energy. Funnily enough, his eyes reminded me of my own. I remembered the quote from the Bulgarian journalist again, about the importance of the gaze of the person. I wondered what this person's voice sounded like.

My initial intuitive response was so strong that I felt physically excited and intrigued. Naturally, I swiped right, and I remember how much I hoped for him to swipe right too — so that we can have a match and be able to text each other on Tinder. And then I actually left my phone and started doing some housework, as it felt pointless to continue swiping at this point. I tried not to think about exactly why I did this, but it just felt right to put the phone down and stop seeking.

My reasoning must have been that I wouldn't be able to find a better profile on Tinder anyway. But my emerging feeling of excitement was indicating something more than that.

I initially ignored it probably because I didn't want to get disappointed if my intuition turned out to be wrong for the first time ever. Later in the same evening, I would check continuously if we had a match, and looked at his pictures over and over again. I didn't want to assume anything at this ridiculously early stage, but I did acknowledge my interest and took it into account.

On the next morning, we had a match. He was actually the first one to text me immediately after we had matched. It was an unexpected ice-breaking joke, to which I actually laughed. I responded in turn, and before we knew it, we exchanged jokes, pictures, memes and references without stopping. At one point it became so weird how we finished each other's sentences and jokes that I had this bizarre feeling that he had access to my head. There was just no other explanation how he responded exactly as I would.

Funnily enough, one of his jokes right after I thought about this was that I must have been spying on him to respond in the exact same way he would. From the outside, this may seem as nonsensical or nothing special, but it felt mesmerising to me. Our communication had such a flow which I never thought possible. It almost felt like an eruption — as if both of us had been piling up some precious data over the years and were just waiting for the right person and time to get it all out, in a creative and insightful way.

We would text each other for hours, in the course of days and weeks. We found each other on Facebook, and I deleted my Tinder profile. When I had access to his Facebook profile, I felt like a kid in a candy store. There were so many interesting shared publications, videos, jokes, more pictures and information about him. I played his music videos over and over, and over again. He had the most appealing voice I had ever heard; quite strong and expressive too. He didn't tell me that he beatboxed as well, which was fascinating to me to see in his videos. I couldn't believe that a human being can do that with his mouth — he was quite good at it as well.

And then there was his published visual art. I couldn't explain it in any other way than he had actually painted my inner world. So many familiar shapes and shades that they actually brought scattered memories of painfully similar abstract and sci-fi paintings, from my old attempts at art. I saw that he had studied at the National Academy of Arts — the university that I had some yearnings to study at myself, but just wasn't good enough. I wondered if we would have met there anyway if I hadn't been so negligent of my visual art talents and had actually been accepted. But then again, it wouldn't have been the right time, I thought.

I also noticed how his character and utilised talents were my own but only in another parallel universe almost — in which I had chosen a different path to develop my gifts and strengths. I wondered if he felt the same way about my characteristics as well. From the way we communicated I felt how similar our inner worlds were, but at the same time how differently and complementarily we had chosen to express them in the outer world. Even though it was just the beginning, I could already vaguely grasp how he might actually have the keys to my locks and the locks to my keys, and vice versa.

TESTING NEVER HURTS

My inner Voice was telling me to go "all in", but that didn't mean that I wasn't cautious or was in a hurry to fall head over heels for someone I still hadn't met in person. He lived in a different Bulgarian city. Having travelled through pretty much the whole of Europe in every method possible, it wasn't a challenge for me to just get up and go visit him, even right away.

But I didn't want to rush it; I needed to put him under a test first to make sure (a little plot twist, later on he told me that he'd been testing me too!). It was just too good to be true, as much as I hate that expression. For all I knew, he could have turned out to be some con artist or psychopath who was a genius in manipulation and knew exactly what to say in order to be liked. Chances were low, but still.

I knew that he was a deep soul too, so gradually I urged our conversations towards more profound and serious topics. We started speaking on the phone and Skype instead of texting, which was a pure gift for me — and from the looks of it, it was for him too. I loved listening to him talk, as his voice was warm and welcoming, but strong at the same time. Since he was a singer and musician, his voice would somehow come out in flow as if he was singing. Soon after, we started making video calls as well — I felt anxious about this at the beginning; after all this was quickly becoming a very important relationship for me. But he would always find a way to break the ice with his characteristic jokes, making me feel at ease in my silly insecurities immediately.

In our all-night-long conversations, we would share our deep values and beliefs, and we would find them matching on 100%. I was astonished how he would get everything that I was talking about and would further contribute with new knowledge that I had not received before from any other source. Our conversations were like a balanced game — the ball was fifty percent of the time in my court, and fifty percent in his. I was in awe of how confidently he would talk about the Light and the inspirations that came from it — even more confidently than me.

We would have so much in common that it was actually bizarre. When he told me his story of going back from Germany to Bulgaria alone on foot and by hitchhiking, I was exhilarated. He was surprised by my excitement and told me that everyone else thought he was crazy because of this adventure he had. In laughter, I told him that I had numerous stories like this — long walking from one country to another, hitchhiking and finding friends and foes on the way — almost like the parables you would find in old philosophical texts. He smiled and nodded, as he knew exactly what I meant. The travelling challenges and survivals in nature held a great meaning to him, just as they did to me.

At that moment, I had the urge to ask him, hesitantly but boldly, the last and ultimate question of my test — "So do you believe in... a higher power then?"

His answer was more ideal than I had imagined: "You mean God?"

"Yes."

"From everything that you've learned about me, what do you think? It's impossible for me not to KNOW about God's existence."

Upon his answer, I immediately felt warmth embracing my soul. I was full of gratitude, inner knowing, and sudden excitement for the future. He had passed all of my tests brilliantly, without trying and even knowing I had been testing him.

An associated memory appeared in my mind at that moment, of an interview with Carl Jung in his late years of life. The psychologist and mystic was asked by the reporter, "Do you now believe in God?" and he answered:

"I don't believe. I know."

BRING YOURSELF TO ACTION

Nearly two months had passed since our initial Tinder match, and then texts, talks and tests. It was time to finally meet in person and both of us felt the urgency. We hadn't exchanged any lovers' messages in our virtual communication, as we had merely explored each other's characters, interests, and values — more like friends. However, we both felt this excitement and longing for affection, and this could be sensed in the tension during our latest conversations.

Naturally, both of us realised the weight of these things and how they have to be kept for after the encounter; they shouldn't be given freely on the internet as something light and casual, because they lose their meaning if the person is not there with you. We had exchanged our views about love and romantic relationships, and they had also matched on 100%. I actually found out that he used to be in an unfitting relationship too and made a promise that he wouldn't let it happen anymore. He'd been searching for his soulmate on Tinder as well, which warmed my heart but at the same time filled me with nervousness and doubts.

"What if I'm not good enough? What if he deserves something better? What if I waste his time too? I do have my weird side, so what if he doesn't accept it, or finds it repulsive? What if my intuition was wrong and he actually isn't the one for me?"

My doubts even included more superficial questions like

"What if he's not as tall as he appears in the pictures?" or "What if he finds me uglier in person than I am in my pictures?"

If you've ever had similar quibbling doubts, you need to know that they are a pitiful attempt by your shadow to prevent you from being brave, letting go of your ego, and doing the right thing. I knew it at that time too, but I still postponed our encounter in time. He suggested coming over for a visit, but I refused a couple of times. I wanted to seize the right moment so that everything would be perfect, and I just didn't feel it. I also had bigger problems at work than usual, and was extra busy, sometimes during the weekends too.

Of course, being extremely intuitive too, he sensed my pitiful doubts from my shadow, and attacked them with the pure energy of his utmost values. He posed a challenge before me. He said:

"If you find something that's worth it, you need to fight for it, and not expect it served on a plate."

By hearing this, my senses were awakened from the slumber and I remembered my core values immediately, as I shattered my pitiful gnawing doubts. He was absolutely right. And with this he helped me realise that we should create that right moment and not wait for it to come on its own, because it never will.

I took a breath and regained my confidence and strength. I surprised him by taking the initiative myself. I made my plans to go visit him in the upcoming weekend. He had already planned to go into the mountains with his friends, but he rescheduled with everyone so that we could meet.

And so there I was on the train to his city Plovdiv, the second biggest city in Bulgaria and one of the most ancient and beautiful places in our home country. It was a Saturday afternoon right before the Sunday of Easter — and I was filled with nervousness and excitement I had never experienced before, not even on my first day of school. I had a clear sense of the importance of this event, and during the train trip, I was reassessing my life until that point. I was already aware that my ultimate choice in life is upcoming, which brought me tension. However, I could also feel a lot of help from the Source, as well as a promise of forthcoming relief.

And so, I prayed. I prayed for it to be just as it should be. Even if he turned out to be someone else and not my soulmate, I would be able to find the strength within and continue searching for the One. By thinking this, I had the nagging feeling from the Voice that I wasn't correct in even considering this option. But I wanted everything to be fair and stable; and if there was going to be any imbalance, I would detect it immediately and take it into account.

"To know each other we must reach beyond the sphere of our sense perceptions." — Nikola Tesla

I also prayed that if he was indeed the One, just as I had felt, to have the magical evening of connection with my kindred spirit that I would never forget.

My train arrived. I was in Plovdiv. We had agreed for him to pick me up from the train station, and I had no more time to think, and overthink. Perhaps, I was taking things again far more seriously than they actually were anyway.

"Here we go," I said to myself, and stepped out of the train.

EMBRACE THE MAGIC

He was late.

I had been waiting for him for twenty minutes already which felt like forever; and just as I was starting to think that it had all been a lie, or a distasteful joke, there I saw him. I recognised him from a distance walking towards me. He had his guitar on his back, and he wore that wide smile with the same small gap between his front teeth that I had found so charming on video. I just couldn't be angry with him that he was late on our first official date, after months of waiting.

We were just super thrilled to finally meet. We began laughing and exchanging jokes immediately; we were so very loud and expressive that people were looking at us strangely as we were walking along the streets of Plovdiv. But we didn't care. It made an impression on me right from the beginning how we skipped all initial awkward moments as if awkwardness never existed on planet Earth. We directly entered our own world of ideas, connections, symbols, metaphors and jokes, which we had created together. It was only our first date and for some reason I already had that "us against the world" type of feeling.

We both had these overflowing energies that would charge from one another, as we continued our flow of inspiring conversations. As he was sharing his stories, I would think about at least ten different things at the same time, which included: "Oh my God, his eyes shine even brighter in person!", "I have never felt so energised by a person before; usually people drain me", "He is so unique and different. I have never met any person in my life that resembles him even a little... except for me, that is" and "I could have conversations like this forever".

As he was walking me through the beautiful touristic sites of Plovdiv, it made an impression on me how we were walking in synchrony, and how he was just as tall as he should be, standing next to me. He asked me what I wanted us to do. I said I didn't mind, although I was secretly hoping that he wouldn't take me to boring cafés or restaurants, like how dates usually go (at least that's how I'd seen them in the movies).

He probably read my mind, which was something quite usual at this point, and said:

"We could go to a restaurant... or we could just go on one of the city hills and play the guitar?"

My face had probably lit up at the second option, because he said, "Well, second option it is."

And so he took me to the highest city peak of Plovdiv. As we were climbing higher and higher, he would offer me a hand to pass through protruding stones and steps. It felt like a dance, and I felt graceful and protected next to him. I would never feel too feminine in other circumstances but with him right there and then, I felt like his feminine half. Also, for some reason I felt that I could achieve anything and everything, if he was always going to be there to offer me a hand in the face of any obstacles.

We reached the spot in which we could see the whole city lit up in the night. It had already become dark, and the spring breeze had a very pleasant sensation on our skins. It was super quiet with no people around — as if we had escaped from the city, and yet the city was there at our feet, looking more welcoming and beautiful than ever.

As I do with everything, I took this event symbolically as well. He had decided to take me to the highest point of the city, from which all the lights could be seen. Our vibrations had become even higher owing to our encounter, and he had probably felt that we wouldn't belong in a crowded place with eating and drinking people, not even in the city park.

When our hands touched accidentally, a little spark came off in a tiny shock. Maybe it was just static electricity from our clothing. Or maybe it was something more, confirming our overflowing matching energies from within.

His idea to bring me there was genius, and I was embracing the magic of the moment as if there was no tomorrow. He took out his guitar and started playing and singing. I had listened to him playing before numerous times on his videos, but this was something different. He was right next to me and I could hear his voice directly, without the barrier of technology. I closed my eyes. I visualised figures of light and various colours and shapes flowing in my mind, as he played the different tunes and sang in perfect harmony with his powerful voice. What I thought impossible was actually happening — my inner world was becoming even more colourful and enriched when I was next to him.

I couldn't believe how surreal all of this was and I asked myself if I was overestimating it. But then I laughed quietly, because my intuition had never been more in tune with my whole being than it was at this very moment. I didn't even have to go inside this time to make sure, as the Voice inside me had become my whole essence at this little point in time.

I had the urge to start singing with him, although a bit

quietly at first because I wasn't sure. He encouraged me and we started singing together in tune. He smiled and said:

"You have talent; I knew it."

"I don't know... Thank you, but how come you knew, though?"

"You see, I have this theory. People like us are gifted with at least one talent. No need to be shy. Oftentimes it's even multiple things! It's because we appreciate the talents God gifted us with, and we develop them accordingly. We have this creative energy. And with you — I already knew that you could paint, and write... and it was very logical that you could sing too, and probably play an instrument as well..."

"That's right! I used to play the piano and compose, but it was a long time ago..."

"It doesn't matter, it still counts. I will help you get back to your talents and put them to good use, even if you have left them behind," he said and smiled, a warm flame dancing in his eyes.

I smiled back and my eyes watered a bit in tenderness. "Thank you."

"Hey, no need to thank me. I know you, so..."

I know you, so... He didn't finish his sentence, but he didn't need to. He wasn't mistaken, he truly knew me. He was probably the only person on Earth at that moment who actually knew the real me.

He just continued playing the guitar and singing, as he would choose my favourite acoustic rock songs. The ones that I used to listen to during my moments of self-reflection and visualisations of my soulmate. I took that symbolically, too, and found it ironic but also kind of sweet. No coincidence could surprise me anymore at this point.

I just felt comfortable, pure and accepted in his company. Instinctively, I rested my head onto his shoulder.

He stopped playing. Everything was quiet again. I said: "I am sorry. I just like it here."

He made a pause, and then rested his head onto mine in return. I could feel his smile when he answered:

"Then you can stay here for as long as you like..."

...and so I did. I stayed.

I had truly found the yang to my yin and the yin to my yang. I... We... had truly finally found the perfect balance and were ready to be transformed together...

"I melted into the dream as if I had always been there. I knew where I had come from; I knew where I was going." — Chelsie Shakespeare

IGNITION PHASE II
TRANSFORMATION

PREPARE FOR TRANSFORMATIONS

"One soulmate is enough to overcome ten thousand soul enemies." — Matshona Dhliwayo

Starting a life together with your partner will inevitably lead to the biggest changes. Luckily, if you really are with the right person, your soulmate, all of these changes will be positive. You will feel your life getting better every day and if you had doubts before, they will gradually be shattered one by one.

Even if you have done wonderful soul work individually and have attracted the right partner, the real growth has yet to begin. That is because the deepest healing is done in partnership, and not just with anyone — but with your soulmate. The purpose of this two-hearted journey is growth and exploration of new possibilities which are only unlocked when you have found your person. The purpose is also to gradually let go of any emotional baggage that might be remaining from any past relationship. Ultimately, this becomes not a journey of two, but a journey of one.

Your soulmate will challenge you to make the right decisions with every hardship that comes your way, and you will challenge them too. This will lead you both to unprecedented transformation, as you will imperceptibly become one super being with a shared arsenal of strengths. As trust is quickly built, your soulmate will become that one person who accepts you to the fullest and to whom you can always go to for consolation and support. You will be the same safe lighthouse for them too.

You may be thinking "that's what best friends are for!" and you will be partly right; however, the soulmate relationship goes far beyond that and transcends. In this physical world it manifests as an expressive energy that emanates from both of you, blends in and creates something beautiful that remains in time. It could be just one thing or multiple things for one lifetime.

For example, creating a family together with your soulmate is magic on its own. I have yet to experience this blessing but I know it's true and I have seen it. The children of two kindred souls carry on the cells of harmony inherited by their parents. The environment in which they grow is also peaceful and stable. This combination of nature and nurture builds up their value systems from early on. The positive model becomes transferrable and they don't need to search for so many answers on their own. They already know what the model of happiness looks like and build on top of that.

Since there isn't an emotional burden from the parents to deal with, the children have the chance to rather focus on developing their strengths, interests and talents from early on. Of course, they should receive the right amount of support they need from their parents — as well as the right amount of scolding, if they start acting a bit spoiled. They also have the safe and solid ground to fall on, if they lose their way by any chance.

More often than not, the two soulmates who have found each other have the urge to create something more together, apart from family. This could be a common business, a mutual creation of art, or just a series of adventures and explorations together. The possibilities are endless; there are no limits in which the two kindred souls will dance together, like the merged flame of two close candles.

A great example of that would be the immensely successful mutual business of Jon and Missy Butcher — two soulmates with a shared vision. Together they created Lifebook, a uniquely designed platform for personal development, spiritual growth, freedom and prosperity in life. They describe it as "a one-of-a-kind lifestyle design system that guides you towards your personal vision of success in the twelve dimensions of life".

While already transforming the lives of millions of users, Jon and Missy are the epitome of two idealists with a common mission, who were firstly transformed by each other's encounter. I could only imagine the passion and the ingenuity with which they initially brainstormed together, while everything was still a single shared idea between them, a shared creative energy.

The pure intentions of their mission must also be taken into account. They worked hard to create this product with the sole purpose of helping souls all over the world to achieve their missions. The couple has also embraced prosperity and has inevitably gained a lot of money on the way; but this wealth is deserved and represents the sweet fruit from hard work over the years, and of their choice to walk steadily on the 8th path.

You see, you don't need to become world-famous personal growth teachers with your soulmate, or creators of a huge billion-dollar product. Unless this is your shared mission, and you develop it together accordingly. But there are countless other ways in which you can merge your creative energies and develop something beautiful. There are no wrong choices if the activity helps you both achieve your pure purposes. The rule is simple: the activity must push you to apply your talents to their ultimate value, as you work in collaboration on the way.

The publishing of this book was encouraged by none other than my soulmate, as I didn't want to do it at first. It is rather personal and all of the stories I share are real and part of my own life, or of people I know. However, he was insistent that if the book helps even one person, it will all be worth it. He inspired me and I agreed. Furthermore, he suggested that he should be the one to make the illustrations, being a freelance graphic designer and illustrator amongst all else. I loved the idea and embraced it immediately. The blending of our two creative soulmate energies happened very intuitively; and this book is a product of both artistic expressions merged into one pure mutual idea: to help people.

***

As a child I knew a very interesting elderly couple living in a small green village right next to my hometown. They were incomparable to any other couple I knew at the time. They were friends to my family, and we would go visit them as guests in their reclusive home outside town, close to nature.

I could only describe their living space as a personal paradise that they had created together. As a child, I could literally sense the harmony and peacefulness of the environment, along with the warmth and cosiness of the reclusive life. In fact, I loved spending time in their house so much that I didn't want to go home even after a long visit. My grandmother and mother would joke that they would leave me there; and I thought how I actually wouldn't mind spending a couple of months there in peace.

They were both people of art. The man wrote poetry which I enjoyed listening to even as a child because it was very pure and included the symbolism of nature and spirit. He was also a craftsman — a carpenter and woodcarver. Their entire home was full of beautiful wood handworks, part of the reason why it was so warm and cosy. He would design some of those works for sale, and others just for his family. His customers loved his work and would say that they could feel his pure spirit alive in his art.

What impressed me the most about this, however, is that he would proudly share how his wife was the one who had encouraged him to start doing woodwork in the first place. He had a muse for it out of the blue — even though he had never done it before. He used to be in the military for years before that, following his father's steps, and not his own path. He disliked it immensely. But then he had his early retirement in his late forties, and they moved away from city life and into nature. Their children were already young adults at that point. They would remain in the city and visit their parents in the village frequently.

So it was after the couple had moved to a more peaceful and fulfilling life that his creative energy made its way through — after years of suppression and distractions. Moreover, his soulmate was the one who encouraged him to make art, just for the sake of art. And he had gotten so good at it over the years that they actually made a decent living out of it. He had become renowned in woodcarving. Naturally, it wasn't a big profit. The greatest wealth he received was the happiness he brought to his customers. And as if that wasn't beautiful enough, he would print out his nice poems and give them out freely as a bonus to go along with the preordered wood-carved products.

As for her, she was a musician. She could play on string instruments beautifully and had composed some of her own melodies. Her husband had learned how to make music instruments out of wood and cords, just to create her very own mandolins and tambourines (both typically Balkan instruments). I don't know if it was my own imagination, but I would find the sound of those handmade instruments magical. Maybe because I knew that he had put his heart into creating them especially for her, and that she had found her muse in music because of him too.

In addition to that, she had the muse to start painting in her latest years. He would create the canvas for her and she would paint all types of nature sceneries and also colourful abstract expressions. They had a lot of those abstract paintings hanging from the walls, and also piled up in their atelier. The paintings were always meaningful to me. I would make my own interpretations of the moods, the emotions or the parts of the human soul that each piece expressed. She would sell a very small number of these paintings, as she would rather give them as gifts to her beloved family and friends. She had given several of those to us as well, in her gratitude that we were her friends.

They were indeed a truly happy couple. They would encourage each other's talents, strengths and positive transformations, as they would face any problem, illness or accident together in perfect attunement. They were also quite spiritual and perpetually seeking, even in their old age — what more could be done to enrich their souls and help them become even better people, until the very end. They looked quite young as well, because their mutual energy was strong, youthful and pure; and the flames in their eyes were such of young people, especially when they laughed heartily.

You see, their experience was very intimate and reclusive, as they had a handful of true friends and small circles of acquaintances and customers. You would never hear about these two soulmates, if I didn't tell you their story. They weren't as successful or as popular as Jon and Missy, but they had everything. And I truly believe they achieved their purposes. I know that their grandchildren are healthy and fulfilled now, all grown up and have started their own happy families.

I also know that this particular couple unintentionally left a sparkle of inspiration and hope in me when I was a child. Just by showing me their example, they opened my eyes. They made my life more exciting knowing that there was indeed a possibility of another family model, and all is a matter of choice. That on its own should be enough to state that these two soulmates have fulfilled their missions and have used their talents for good — by lighting nothing but a single sparkle into a young inexperienced soul.

POSITIVE AFFIRMATIONS

There is another distinguishable trait that all soulmate relationships have in common. The same could be easily seen with the elderly couple too. It is the positive affirmations with which the kindred souls express their love and appreciation for one another, over and over again. The more these affirmations are repeated, the stronger the bond gets. Additionally, the flame grows bigger even after a long period of time; and the relationship gets purified on a regular basis — because to show and confirm love means to leave your heart open and vulnerable, but to trust your partner at all times. When love is returned back, it enriches this flame between the two, and it never dies.

"Sometimes soul bonds are stronger than blood bonds. Have faith in that." — Dianna Hardy, *Aftershock*

Those positive affirmations always come from the heart and are unique for every couple. They could be related to the way your partner brings you joy after a hard day at work, or how they perfectly complement your ideas when the two of you are speaking to other people. It could be anything from acknowledging the smallest gestures, to confirming your overall perfect compatibility. No matter what it is, positive affirmations never get old and are always a good thing to do.

But why, you may ask. Because they are an act of thankfulness. Together with love and faith, thankfulness is one of the healthiest and purest states of mind you can ever have.

When you are thankful to your partner, you inevitably appreciate them more and you never take them for granted. You know that they work to enrich this relationship just as much as you do. This fairness makes you feel at peace and full of gratitude.

In this way, you are also more perceptive of their positive side — their strengths and how they apply them in your relationship, and generally in life. You know your partner more deeply every day, and you continue to see the patterns of similarity between them and yourself. You begin to see your own self in a better light too, as you receive these positive affirmations back. You feel your transformation into a better human being taking place in real time. This alone is your gift of happiness, as the feeling is indescribable. It would not be possible in any other relationship, even in the case of best friends.

"It is an absolute human certainty that no one can know his own beauty or perceive a sense of his own worth until it has been reflected back to him in the mirror of another loving, caring human being." — John Joseph Powell, *The Secret of Staying in Love*

There is another side of this thankfulness too. By being thankful in your relationship, you send off a particular signal of gratitude to a higher dimension too. You are in a sense thankful to none other than God, for bringing you together with your dear kindred spirit. You realise that you have had the chance of achieving such privilege, because you have worked on your growth very diligently. And now you are picking the sweet fruit of that hard work.

Don't be thrifty with your thankful words to the Source — in a way, they are positive affirmations too. Be grateful for everything He has given you and say it openly in prayer over and over again. Even for the smallest things — acknowledge them, be grateful, and thank your Creator. He wants you to be happy and fulfilled and be in tune with what your true heart desires. So when he sees your whole essence filled with gratitude, this is an endearing gift returned back to Him.

The positive affirmations are indeed intimate in their nature but could partly be shared with the closest circles of the couple too. The woodcarver from the elderly couple proudly shared how his wife was supportive with his art ventures. You can hear in his voice how he was filled with joy, tenderness and gratitude. The most perceptive people from your friends and family will pick up this light of thankfulness. Hopefully, they will take from it and apply it to their unique experience — without really stealing anything from you, since you'd be giving it freely.

You might refresh the vision of some couples in this way, as you let them see what a true kindred relationship looks like. But be careful: others might hate you for the same reason or be jealous of you. You have to know that this doesn't affect you in any way and it is their own choice. If your intentions are entirely pure and your words are devoid of bragging, everything should be fine.

However, it is your responsibility to have awareness, and not share anything in too much detail. Don't kill the magic by sharing it all publicly, and don't rub it off. Don't feed your ego in this reckless way, after all the hard work you've done to tame it down. Remember, there is a reason why the positive affirmations are intimate in their nature, and predominantly expressed within the couple's own private space. Moreover, the positive affirmations always, and I repeat always, must come from the heart and not be forced — no matter if they are exchanged between the partners, or shared with the outside world.

Additionally, everyone goes through their own stages of spiritual growth, and romantic relationships are a good indicator of where the soul is at currently. You can't pull the person by force and match them with their soulmate against their will and at the wrong time. Everyone has their own unique lesson to learn in the school of life. Everything must happen organically through their own journey of realisations, shadow work, humility, growth and seeking. You can only be their wise advisor to some extent, if they open their hearts to you and say, "Teach me how to have what you have." This might indicate their readiness or upcoming readiness in the following years.

Even in this case, be cautious of how you give advice. Take into account that while many of the soulmate relationships have a lot of things in common, they are also largely unique as well — as individuals we have no equivalents in our precise design. Thus, your advice might be fruitless to the other person, because it will be taken from your own experience. After all, the person you give advice to will have their own mistakes to make and lessons to learn, as well as a very unique purpose; and not to be overlooked, a pace that is different from your own.

This is why it is important for everyone to know themselves first and to know what makes them unique. So that they can figure out the rest of the answers largely on their own. In this way, a person won't need strict advice from other soulmates on how to execute a strategy; but will rather find his or her own way to the 8th path intuitively — and through a lot of individual inner work. We have already discussed how there is not one single right way to find your soulmate, as there is not a single right way to do shadow work or to find God.

What you can do for the Greater good, however, is to live your life with your partner to the fullest. To fulfil your truest potentials and create something beautiful together that will last in time. This alone will light sparkles here and there, as other people will notice that and be amazed by it. They will come to you on their own for knowledge and comfort; as you will give them nothing but a single light of hope and a warm feeling of true home, through your own unique example.

TRUE LOVE MEANS RECIPROCITY

"True love is not a hide and seek game: in true love, both lovers seek each other." — Michael Bassey Johnson

I watched a video on YouTube of Matthew Hussey — a British life coach and love expert who regularly organises interactive sessions with audiences. A guy from the audience named Roy asked Matthew a question: "My ex moved on fast. It hurts, man. We were together for five... six years. And when they move on fast, it makes you feel that you're not good enough, you know. How do I change my perspective so that I can learn how to let go?"

Matthew made a pause and thought about his words carefully. What he answered was very wise and contained several important truths. I will always remember his exact words and give his advice to people going through the same difficulties.

"Roy, you are going through an incredible amount of hurt. It is incredibly painful. Part of the pain is you continuing to convince yourself that this must, on some level, have been the right person. And that your right person is now with someone else. Now I don't believe that. I believe that the right person can only be the right person when it's two people choosing each other.

"So part of the pain we hold on to is believing still that we had this 'jewel' that's gone. And as much as we may have loved someone, as much as we may have thought someone was incredible — they may have had wonderful qualities, we may have been incredibly attracted to them, they may have been all these great things — they cannot represent that true dream relationship, if they don't choose you.

"In fact, someone not choosing you is just about the biggest departure from your dream relationship you could ever imagine. So when we're saying 'but we were so close!', not being chosen by someone should be the greatest turn-off in the world. Not because there's something wrong with that person, but because how on earth, when I was a kid and I dreamt about my dream relationship, it couldn't have been the one where someone decides to go be with someone else. That wasn't it! So this isn't it.

"… then there's the ego. The ego element of someone choosing someone else. Why not me? What did that person have, why wasn't I good enough? And now we take the baggage of that forward. The greatest advice I ever received was 'Kill. Your. Ego.' Because that has no place in your growth. None.

"We're all going to die — many, many times in our lives. You just died! A piece of you has to die. Right now, you're going through hell. It's been awful, someone ripped your heart out — that's hell. But I want that version of you that goes through hell and comes out and has something to say at the end of it. Do I want the version of Roy who hasn't been through that? Nah, it's boring. I don't want that Roy. I want Roy who's been to hell and back. I want Roy who had to die, resurrect himself, and then come and tell the rest of us how to do that!"

Very strong quote. And Matthew is right. Your soulmate will never make you go through hell. They will never make you suffer or choose someone else. Forget phrases like "true love always hurts". No, it doesn't. Opposites don't attract, either — forget that. In my ten years of investigation of personality psychology, I have never encountered a concept which suggests that two people have the exact opposite personalities — after all, personality is not a bipolar magnet; it's far more complex than that. Even if you theoretically find that "opposite" person, do you really think it would be a successful relationship?

Your true soulmate chooses you because the two of you are alike. Your soul frameworks are the same, but each fills the gaps a bit differently with their own experience. This is why being with someone like you is never boring, counter to some beliefs. After you equalise your frequencies, which happens very quickly with a soulmate, they charge each other into a hundred times stronger channel of energy, instead of just two times. That's because there is a perfect match in the electric currents. Additionally, you can learn everything by being with your alternative self in a way, who has the same matrix but has chosen a slightly different path from your own. It is almost as if you're cheating the game and you have two life experiences instead of just one.

Your soulmate chooses you because they see you as a mirror; and they wouldn't make any other choice in the world from the point they have discovered their reflection. Your soulmate makes a vow to never let go, not because they have to — but because they are aware that you are their ideal match and stand above every other potential half-suited relationship. Your soulmate chooses you because they know that you have chosen them too; and thus, the two of you form an enclosed system.

Your soulmate never makes you chase them; they might challenge your idleness and lack of initiative, but they never play games with you. They give just as much as you do to enrich the relationship, and they love it. You don't really count that in a soulmate relationship; it all happens naturally and intuitively. You don't fight with your soulmate about how one partner has contributed more than the other. Both sides are readily willing to give, and they do it out of pure love and gratitude. This creates abundance and there is never any scarcity in the relationship.

True love means reciprocity. Both of you recognise each other as the One. There is no perfect person, but there is a person who is perfect for you. What makes them perfect for you, apart from their wondrous qualities and their matching personality to yours, is the fact that they chose you and they would do it all over again, and again, in another lifetime.

This is the power of choice. It could be applied to all truths, and especially the one related to reciprocity. Just as in mathematics, reciprocity holds true in human relationships too, because it is all part of a Divine law. Always be thankful to your soulmate about the choice they made with you. This could be one of your most powerful positive affirmations.

Thank God too for allowing you to experience the manifestation of His Divine law of reciprocity, by providing you with requited soulmate love.

TRUE LOVE MEANS SHARING

"It's not the way they taught us. They didn't know the formula for love. One plus one actually equals one. 1+1=1." — Kate McGahan, *One Heart's Journey*

After a couple of years of being together with my soulmate and sharing everything, some people became sceptical and started asking us questions like: "Don't you ever get tired or bored with each other?"

Even though they are outsiders to our relationship and their opinion is subjectively based on their own experiences, I understand where they're coming from. Since we got together, we have been together nonstop — we have been travelling together, have taken summer jobs together at the Bulgarian seaside; we moved in together in Plovdiv almost immediately. Going out with friends, we're always together. It makes sense, because since we are so alike, we also like the same type of people. So naturally, his pack of best friends became my pack almost instantly — and vice versa. We have always cherished our cosy moments together at home as well, practising our creative hobbies in pure harmony, or just watching stupid shows and laughing together. When we visit my family in my hometown, we always go together as one unseparated whole.

There is hardly any moment in which we are not by each other, and this may seem strange to outsiders. It may seem as if we're "trapped" into this smothering relationship and there is no way out. It is natural to think and feel this way if you have never been with your soulmate. Being with anyone else for too long at a time smothers you and drains you at one point. If there is no deep intimacy, the couple starts losing passion, connection, and the partners begin to slowly experience the relationship as a mere chore and duty. Chore and duty. This is when the love dies — if it ever truly existed, that is.

When you are with the One, it's something completely different. You feel this excitement and joy in sharing with them everything you've discovered about life so far. You're almost in the state of impatience to show them your most valuable experiences — because at the times you had those experiences, you had no one to share the moments with. So you open up to your kindred spirit like a book: with all of your sincerity, excitement and vulnerability. And they do the same thing. It is the greatest feeling when you share a deeply cherished childhood memory with someone, and they listen closely and respond with the voice of your heart.

I want you to remember a very touching moment in your life, which was very special to you — but you didn't share it with anyone, or maybe you shared it with the wrong person. Now imagine getting together with this right person and telling them the story of this special moment. They listen attentively and emerge into your memory visually, getting to know you even better by recreating all the beautiful details of imagery in their head. After you've shared your story, your partner is touched as well, because he or she has relived this cherished moment with you — even though they had no chance of being with you right then and there. I pray with all my heart that you experience such moments of shared magic, and I hope that you have experienced it already as you are reading this.

Being with the One, changes your perspective on

relationships and on personal space. Even if you are a hardcore introvert such as myself, your soulmate will be the only person who doesn't drain you. On the contrary — they will supply you with energy, and the purest energy there is. When you become one with them, you almost feel a part of you missing, when they are away for a week. You are still well and strong, but you have this healthy and sweet longing for your other half. This is how strong the bond is, and this is how irrelevant the "standard" relationship advice gets. Recommendations like "it's good for the partners to be away from each other for longer periods of time" or "it's good for the partners to fight in order to keep the spark alive" become totally and utterly ridiculous.

"I laugh harder with you. I feel more myself with you. I trust you with me — the real me. When something goes wrong, or right, or I hear a funny joke, or I see something bizarre, you're the first person I want to talk to about it." — Samantha Young, *Before Jamaica Lane*

It is very important to keep the childlike state of the relationship. This excitement of sharing actually resembles very much the bond of two children who have just become friends. They feel so thrilled that there is another kid they could share their interests with — play with each other's toys, show the cartoons and comics they've previously seen just on their own, etc. Sharing each other's "gems" is the greatest way to fortify your mutual trust — just like a well-built Lego castle constructed by two children working together, rather than a weak castle built by a lonely child. It is not by chance that childhood friendships that survived in time are oftentimes the strongest and purest friendship bonds of all. When your bond is built inside this childlike state of sharing, it remains solid and untainted no matter what happens in life after that.

These "gems" sometimes include precious friendships as well. You have this childlike impatience to have your soulmate meet this or that person, because you are sure that they will like each other. I've actually had some great rekindling of lost friendships because I wanted to acquaint those people with my soulmate, and they naturally bonded (sometimes even more than me!). And this leads you not only to joy and confirmation of how you two are so alike, but also to the growth of your pack and the positive influence you can have on mutual friends with your relationship.

In parallel to sharing your "gems" from your two separate past experiences, the new challenges come your way waiting for you to deal with them in partnership and sharing again. The more quality time you spend together with your soulmate, the stronger the bond gets and the stronger you become as partners in crime. The joy multiplies when shared, as well as the adventurous spirit. Before you know it, you have enough content to write a whole book with exciting, funny or action stories you have lived through together. You may even go through difficult times together and remain stable only because you have stood together.

Walking hand in hand with your soulmate on the 8th path is exciting, different, funny, interesting, healing, stimulating, invigorating and purifying. Of course, you would want to share pretty much everything from your life with this one person! It may be hard to believe, but it is the truth. I've been in a long mediocre relationship and I know the gap between the two. The difference is like night and day.

Of course, you may have the need for personal space from time to time. But it doesn't exactly feel like the usual vital need for complete disconnection from the outer world. It feels more like a need for a mere introspection and quietness without interaction. And you can have this every day if you want, as the right partner will give it to you freely and will not be demanding. For me, this is the need to concentrate on my projects and to get inside my head. I know that my soulmate is there next to me doing his creative freelance work as well, and we are still in a way together with shared creative energies, but each is doing their own thing. This is a form of personal space.

Another form is for both of you to have your own leisure activities. Sometimes he prefers to play videogames and I prefer to read books, and other times it's the other way around. A third option for us would be to do both things together. It really depends on how we feel it's right. Since we're both very intuitive, we don't need many words of interaction to sense what the other needs and which is the best way to do it this time. You don't have any duties in a soulmate relationship, but you do the right things no matter small or big, merely from the heart.

You also have all the freedom and flexibility in this relationship. For what it's worth, you can go around the world on your own and come back in several years, and your partner will support you in that. They will have plenty of self-respect and trust in you to say yes to all of your ambitions. However, chances are very low that you will want to continue doing such things on your own or with other people, now that you have your kindred spirit next to you. In fact, your first instinct when something new comes into your life is to share it with your soulmate. You are interested in how they see it, and you want to experience life through their eyes as well.

"I would like to travel the world with you twice. Once, to

see the world. Twice, to see the way you see the world." — Unknown writer

There will be plenty of friends for you to interact with, but consciously or subconsciously you will always compare your communications to that perfect one, as no one else will be able to reach it. That doesn't mean that you shouldn't have any friends or any other deep bonds. You must truly love all people and feel compassion for them. However, you should especially cherish your ultimate bond with that one person, and not take it for granted, or sacrifice it for other less ideal relationships.

This is why sharing is the greatest thing you can do for your relationship; and the best thing about it is that it comes lightly and naturally with your soulmate. It rather feels unnatural if you don't share things with your partner. Don't forget that the Voice never leaves your side, and is especially activated in a soulmate relationship, distinguishing right from wrong now more than ever.

As for the other people — they will always talk. And you can't do anything about that. As we have previously discussed, your pure relationship will bring light and knowledge to some awakened or seeking people, but confusion and jealousy to others who are still asleep. And the best path you can always take is to live your dream life with your partner; and allow the rest to sort itself out.

HEAL THROUGH CONFLICTS

"If you make being 'right' more important than maintaining connection, you will never be able to heal and grow through conflict. You will continue to hit the same limits in love, because you aren't willing to surrender your ego, and thereby, further open your heart" — Mark Groves

Even though you are soulmates, that doesn't mean that you won't have conflicts from time to time. It is important to understand what those conflicts represent, and to put a meaning to them before you resolve them successfully in partnership.

Even though your souls are very similar, don't forget that the two of you have been on very different paths before taking the 8th path together, hand in hand. This means that in your individual ways you have stumbled upon different types of challenges and have resolved them in unique ways. Take this as a positive thing. Each soul was coloured by life differently until you were brought together. This variety will help you explore possibilities and ultimately find balance. It will help you understand your slight differences and bring you exactly to the point of that deepest healing that I mentioned earlier.

Most of the time, when we have big problems in life and we are forced to deal with them on our own, we fall back on a palette of unhealthy ways to cope. Some people go into victim mode, others go violent; and I've personally met people who go straight away into depression and reclusion once they face hardship. No matter what the colour or shade of these unhealthy ways, you already know that you are strong enough to heal yourself from this — by doing shadow work and introspection diligently. However, even if you do it right, sometimes there are remainders left in your system; small dark "bugs" that activate from time to time, leading you back to your old models of behaviour which you hate so much. Not too often — but often enough to be in temporary conflict even with your soulmate.

Your kindred spirit can and will help you with that. Because they won't have the same unhealthy ways to cope — these are unique to you — they will notice these "bugs" and will confront them. Hence, the conflict emerges. However, when you are in conflict with your soulmate, you have this feeling that even that is in relation to growth; and you know that it is constructive rather than destructive — once it stops, the relationship will be stronger than ever, and you will go back to your usual positive affirmations.

In this regard, another interesting feeling that you might have while quarrelling with your soulmate is that they have found the deepest shadows of you which you never managed to reach or realise in order to heal. And this is what your partner is for — to make you aware of those unhealed parts and attack them, even though it means a temporary fight. Even if you are fighting, you still feel that your own arguments don't come from your true self, but from those untended wrong models of behaviour; and you feel unnatural while quarrelling with the love of your life, knowing in your heart that they are right.

Your ego will still act up on occasions, and the Voice will alert you about this; continue to listen to the Voice at all times.

The Voice of your soulmate will also allow him or her to see the truth. Sometimes it will not even be about the two of you, but about how one of you treats a family member or a close friend in an unhealthy way. The other partner will notice that and confront the "guilty" party in a loving but strict way. They challenge the guilty party to look even deeper into their own soul and ask the question "Why?" yet again, which will ultimately lead to letting go of ego once more, and get to the deeper healing.

The conflicts with your soulmate are never heart-breaking or hurting. They are enlightening. The quarrelling is the product of remaining emotional baggage from past relationships or unhealthy coping mechanisms, which only your soulmate can lift off your shoulders gradually.

The conflicts with your soulmate are yet another challenge posed in front of you — whether to become a better person and upgrade to the next soul level, or to fall back into your old ways.

The conflicts with your soulmate never last for too long, and do not lead to drama, trauma, or pain. They are ultimately healing of your deepest remainders of shadow. Just as that last scrub you make when you wash the dishes to make them shiningly clean, your soulmate makes an effort to help you become ultimately purified.

The conflicts with your soulmate are very rare, close to non-existent if you've done your soul work correctly. If the conflicts last for too long, or are happening on a frequent basis, it might mean that you still have some individual work to do. If there is pain or grudge left in your heart, after a series of conflicts, it might be a good indicator that this may not be your soulmate. Your real soulmate always acts in your favour as a person, and in the favour of the two of you as a couple. If your real soulmate has resolved to conflict, it means that it is really necessary for your healthy growth. But if the Voice gives you the wrong feelings of hurt and emptiness after a fight, there is truly something wrong.

KEEP ON INTROSPECTING

Exploring the possibilities in your life together is the most exciting thing. But it doesn't rule out your need to continue to self-reflect and analyse your own inner world.

On the contrary, you will clearly see the degrees in which you have transitioned to a better human being, in your relationship dynamic. You will find yourself in tune with your Voice more than ever before. You will start to see the patterns of better choices you have made since you started this relationship. Your shadow will be so obvious to you that at the moment it does manifest, you will be able to cease it immediately and make the decision to feel, think and act inside the light instead.

I remember how several months after our relationship began, I already liked myself better. The real me, that is. I loved the way he made me feel about myself. This may sound egotistical, but it's not. Your soulmate will definitely be there to make you feel better about yourself, apart from everything else. They will after all bring out the best in you, and this will be available for you to observe in your quiet self-reflection moments.

It's not egotistical also because when you like yourself and your light, you burst with happiness and you want to give it out freely — as much as you can, to any soul, and as frequently as you can. You make a stranger's day better with your emanating light, positive energy and kind words. You give compliments just because, and they come from the heart, which activates even for a millisecond the light within the other person as well. Not always, but often enough. The light is more contagious than the shadow because it's far more natural, it feels better, and it gently awakes the somewhat neglected feelings of our real home and self.

The best thing is that this overflowing happiness is really the final product of years of self-work, conscious awareness, seeking, attuning and adapting. What it really shows is how strong you have become. No matter what has happened to you, you have found the way to be uncompromisingly happy and ready to make other people happy all the time. You have also beaten the odds and found just the right person to amplify this happiness in you and for you, even more strongly — making you the closest thing to a superhuman there is.

"The belief that unhappiness is selfless and happiness is selfish is misguided. It's more selfless to act happy. It takes energy, generosity, and discipline to be unfailingly light-hearted." — Gretchen Rubin, *The Happiness Project*

PLAN THE FUTURE

"When I look at her, I see a lot of things: my best friend, my soulmate, my secret holder, my tear stopper, my future." — Arif Naseem

This usually comes very naturally when you are with the One. Visions of different paths you can take together race through your mind, and you become overwhelmed by the possibilities.

One of the functions of your soulmate is to enrich your imagination even more. This will encourage you to daydream, individually or together. At times you will feel that one lifetime is not enough to fulfil all your dreams, to develop all your passions and hobbies, or to do all the pleasant leisure activities you love. But the best thing is that you already fulfilled a big mutual mission just when you found each other.

Your task here is to be a bit more reasonable and think of the ultimate ways to make use of your time together. You won't be living forever on this earth, after all. Consider and plan the best options in which you will combine work with pleasure. Listen to your intuition again, as always. One of the difficulties many soul-mate couples face is rather ironic in its nature: they enjoy each other's company so much that they can't get to work. They prefer living day by day, without savings or long-term plans, so that they can take delight in the present moment. This wears out too quickly, however, as fate slaps them on the face in one way or another.

I knew a couple in their thirties from my university town who were cute as a button. The girl was the big sister of one of my university classmates and this is how I got to know them. They were always together, side by side, always positive and with smiling, shining eyes. They even looked alike physically. Both were tall and skinny, with long and straight blondish hair, often tied in a ponytail, and fair complexion with light greenish eyes. She was a hell of a singer, and he was a guitarist in a band; and this is how they met — through their passion in life, rock music. They also had the coolest style ever — leather jackets, worn-out jeans and all that.

The interesting thing with them was that they never had a real job, even though they were reaching their mid-thirties. They were obviously non-conformists to social norms, and I liked them for that. I guess I always had this rebellious part of me, and it resonated to some extent with their lifestyle back then. They would preach how the soul is the most important thing and selling yourself to a nine-to-five job that you don't like is equal to cheating your nature. And this is how you miss the important moments in life. I would agree with them to a certain extent, but at the back of my mind I would think that maybe this is why it is so important to combine your mission in life with your work — and if it happens to be a nine-to-five job, then so be it.

They would have some band gigs from time to time in famous clubs in Veliko Tarnovo, or play music on the central square for some extra cash from generous tourists. They lived in a tiny old rented room in the outskirts of the city, with a shared bathroom and kitchen. Even though the price of this ditch was extremely low, they would share openly how they were almost kicked out on several occasions because they didn't have money to pay their rent. They would frequently borrow money from their rocker friends, and even from the younger sister of the woman — my classmate.

They were very free-spirited and would go around Bulgaria with trains and buses on trips, because they didn't own a car. They would spend several weeks in the mountains together in a tent, and then they'd go to the seaside for the summer, camping again. For the winter, they would go back to my university town Veliko Tarnovo; and usually the winter months were the hardest for them.

Since they were so interesting to me with their stories and how open they were about everything, I asked my classmate to invite the couple every time we went out with our university group. She didn't mind and invited them several times more. They would always gladly come, especially since they knew that I'd be paying for their pizza and drinks. But I found it funny and charming and didn't judge them for that. I enjoyed listening to their point of view, since it was so different. Furthermore, it appeared to me that they might be soulmates by the way they talked in synchronisation, and had very similar interests, energies and even looks.

They were usually very positive and would proudly and enthusiastically share their different choices from the "average sheep", as they would call "normal" people. They would always emphasise how interesting it was for them to share this journey with each other; and that life is one big adventure that doesn't need planning. The magic happens here and now, they would say, and if you don't capture it, you'll miss it forever. They made themselves sound very confident in their beliefs, although every time I would feel a certain insecurity or shame mixed with anxiety, emerging from their voices and eyes.

On one occasion they told me that they had troubles with drugs once. When I asked them why they even tried them in the first place, the woman responded immediately that it was because of anxiety.

It was one of those harsh winters, and they had no money to pay the rent. They were freezing in their broken ditch, and had no organised gigs or savings to keep them warm and well fed. It was a nightmare, and she began having panic attacks because of anxiety and helplessness.

Naturally, he wanted to help her, so he asked a couple of friends in their rock community. One of them suggested a special "happy pill" that "would push all of the anxiety away", and he took it on trust. It seemed to work, but just as any drug, they would feel ten times worse the day after, and would require more and more after that. They got even deeper in debt because of that. They recovered from this nightmare on their own by using nothing but strength of will; however, it left them traumatised, depressed and bitter for some time after that.

I listened to this story with a mixture of feelings: disbelief, compassion, frustration. I couldn't help but ask them, "What about your future? What about… children?" It may have been a very straightforward and even rude question. But I was just overwhelmed by the arising idea in my head that they were no free spirits. They were rather wasters of their potentials and have even willingly reached one of the lowest points of human existence — drugs. They were also losing precious time in their attempt to not lose time. It was so ironic; so subtly but utterly wrong; and they were already in their mid-thirties, so I just had to ask them, and I couldn't help myself.

I remember what they answered, "We are still… not ready." It bugged me a lot to receive an answer like that. I thought about their example long after I'd met them; and still to this day wonder if they were soulmates or not. They didn't bring the best in each other, and they would close their eyes to the truth. On the other hand, they would support each other in their opinions, and would spend all of their time together in harmony.

Perhaps, they were indeed soulmates who got wrapped up in the moment of their younger lives, the moment of their encounter. And they liked it so much that they wanted to freeze in time, right then and there. I suppose they wanted to live, and relive, the freedom and irresponsibility of youth; forgetting that with maturity also come wisdom, growth, new different experiences, family, and ultimately — legacy.

They didn't take into account that planning for the future is not only a good thing, but it shows the care for each other, and the seriousness of the relationship. Fulfilling your plans together with the love of your life should be your very own pill for anxiety. Planning for the future means that you are ready. Ready for the next stage of life with your partner.

Planning means that you have learned your lessons so far and you are brave enough to go out of your comfort zone once again. Designing your mutual future means taking God's plan for you and your partner seriously, and trying to put it into practice together, in partnership. It also shows how important your soulmate is to you. Planning is the ultimate way to show them that the best is yet to come, but that everything that's happened until now will always remain in your heart, that you will always cherish your most precious memories but are looking forward to making even better ones.

You don't need confirmation that all of your plans will succeed; and you will inevitably experience a certain number of failures and unexpected turns of destiny. You will have to make adjustments on the way, and to adapt accordingly to the circumstances. But that doesn't mean that you shouldn't have a fixed goal in your head, together with the love of your life, and work towards it. It may come true in one way or another, or something even better may come — who knows? But one thing is for sure — you need to work for it honestly, diligently and in partnership with your soulmate.

"Money", "savings", "planning" and "standard day job" are not dirty concepts. If they are done with love and in peace, they will add up to your common arsenal of strengths, will develop your critical thinking and confidence even more, and will earn you respect. There's nothing wrong with that. Of course, if you decide to take the freedom-loving, spontaneous path, that would also be OK. But be aware of the pros and cons of both situations, and especially of the sacrifices you would have to make with your frivolous choice — because it will inevitably affect your active growth, the formation of your family, and your legacy.

"The seeds we sow today will grow to serve as shades for weary travellers tomorrow." — Nike Thaddeus

I have no idea what happened with that rocker couple. They must already be in their early forties now and I hope that they are happy. I secretly hope that they have settled down into a more secure life now, hopefully with a child running around. That's because I want the best for them, and I know that building a home and a family is ultimately the purest and most reasonable choice a couple can make. Because that is what God wants for us too — to be fruitful (in any way) and to multiply. Your intuition has already confirmed this, I am sure.

I pray for their wellbeing and health and will always

remember them as the cool rocker couple, as the two partners in crime who were perfect for each other. With them it was all a matter of awakening, as they were already overflowing with love. I am an idealist and I believe that true love ultimately overcomes all. For me, true love in any shape or form resembles the nature of our Creator; and it is not by chance that it has been repeated many times in the Bible and in our lives, that God is love. If we do work hard to live in love, and we live up to His name, all the little things will be sorted out for us sooner or later.

EMBRACE THE RISKS

"We have to continually be jumping off cliffs and developing our wings on the way down." — Kurt Vonnegut, *If This Isn't Nice, What Is?: Advice to the Young*

As we have discussed, being together with your soulmate enriches your imagination and opens your mind to new possibilities. Your courage and enthusiasm grow as well, especially because it is shared. But sharing your life with your other half also brings you to action. It pushes you to take the lead in your life and make it better for the sake of the two of you, and for those who will come next.

You will be pushed out of your comfort zone many times in your soulmate relationship, leading to your growth. You will be faced with many new choices to make, and some of them will involve taking risks. You have to master the art of risk taking, as it will come in handy when the most fateful choices come. You also have to learn how to be reasonable but also brave with your risks, enriching your passionate nature.

"To live a life of excellence, you will have to take risks. You will have to step into new territory and climb new mountains. If you're up to something that's as big as you are, it's going to be scary. If it feels perfectly safe, you are probably underachieving. To leave your mark in the world, you will have to stand someplace you've never been willing to stand before. And you will have to have the courage to aspire to excellence." — Debbie Ford, *The Best Year of Your Life:*

Dream It, Plan It, Live It

When you have done the most part of the planning with your partner, you must already have an idea of what you want to achieve together in life from now on; how you want to spend your time and resources to leave something meaningful behind. Further brainstorming with your soulmate will provide you the finest details and is actually a very pleasurable activity to do with them.

If you have the idea of building a new business with your partner (or alone), it will involve taking new risks that you might have never encountered before. You need careful planning and maybe a consultation with a specialist with years of experience in the business, who can walk you through the specifics — realistically and practically. Don't be too hasty by letting your shared enthusiasm cloud your judgment and lead you to unnecessary mistakes. Calculate the risk first, and then take it.

If you have the idea of moving to another unknown city (or country) with your partner, first research if the place will provide you both with all the necessary resources for your development and wellbeing. Take the risk of moving only when you have reached absolute harmony with your soulmate, and your choice matches on 100%. You never know what the new life in a bigger city (or in the countryside) has prepared for you, but you can at least take some time to consider the options before making the step.

If you have the idea of taking a loan in order to build a home with your soulmate, or to invest in a business or art project, or to travel the world together, take a deep breath first. When money is involved, the stakes are high, so think about it carefully. This risk's outcome will resonate for years to come, so don't be "in the here and now" but consider the consequences diligently. Many soulmate couples who have just been brought together are still enraptured by the magic of their encounter, and this enthusiasm sometimes brings them to the wrong risks related to money. They want their lives to be sorted out as soon as possible, and they take the shortcut, which isn't a shortcut at all.

Whether it's nicer to be in the clouds, when it comes to taking risks related to money, you need to be on the ground. Consider your priorities before taking a loan or spending your savings. If you have done soul work in the right way, you will already have particular neutrality to material belongings, lux, and convenience. In fact, you might be drawn more to nature and the simple way of life than to any other boastful or lustrous lifestyle. Perhaps, you prefer to concentrate your energy on spiritual growth rather than gaining more and more material belongings. However, bear in mind that it doesn't have to be one or the other — you can achieve both with the right mindset and balance. Happiness can be found within first, and all of your choices will be an extension of that.

By keeping your focus on your ultimate goal and by listening to the Voice, you can always assess the risks correctly — even if they include taking a loan or spending a big amount of money. If this really resonates with your heart and you are prepared to take the consequences in the years to come, take the risk and be happy about it. Once you take it, you need to embrace your choice completely — no regrets or second thoughts, and no transfer of blame. You already know the cost of that. Leave out all the rest to the Source and pray frequently in gratitude and hope. Be passionate and hopeful of the immense goodness you will be rewarded with by taking your risk right now.

"If you imagine less, less will be what you undoubtedly deserve. Do what you love, and don't stop until you get what you love. Work as hard as you can, imagine immensities, don't compromise, and don't waste time. Start now. Not twenty years from now, not two weeks from now. Now."— Debbie Millman

Apart from the material risks you will take, there is a special type of risk that will be essential to your ultimate growth. The risk to always take the high road.

You have already acquired an outstandingly positive mindset through intense shadow work, introspection and conscious growth. And you need to remind yourself that the majority of people are not able to achieve what you have in a whole lifetime. They just refuse to have that awareness.

Thus, you will inevitably find yourself in inconvenient and challenging situations over and over again, to reveal how much you've grown, and yet, how humble you've remained. You will meet people who will consciously or subconsciously try to bring you down emotionally or spiritually. You will see patterns in the repeating archetypes of such people in your life — the gossiping co-worker, the mean boss, the back-stabbing friend, etc. But your mission is to let go of ego, forgive them and still be kind to all of them, no matter what.

Take the risk and choose not to be involved. They may try to make you appear weak or prove that you don't know how to protect yourself. On the contrary — by being unyieldingly kind no matter what, this is how you protect your values and stay true to your purest self. In this way you show that there is no real threat to your beliefs, and that you don't have the need to prove yourself. This is what real strength and self-respect mean. You have heard phrases like "don't fall on their level" and while there is some truth in that, I find that phrase highly condescending. You need to have compassion for all people and always remember that everyone is going through their kinds of inner battles; you need to be humble, and take the risk in loving them all, no matter how they act or how they treat you, or what the consequences might be.

"The high road of grace will get you somewhere a whole lot faster than the freeway of spite." — Aaron Lauritsen, *100 Days Drive: The Great North American Road Trip*

By taking this risk, you will inevitably appear different and stand out. You risk making enemies in such a way because there will be people who don't understand your light and will try to shut it down. Regardless, the risk is absolutely worth it. Only by taking it will you be able to embrace your transformations fully and build your purest connections and relationships too — the ones that you wouldn't be able to build otherwise.

Only by taking the high road can you go further on your ladder to truth, closer and closer to God. Only in this way will you be able to prepare yourself for your third major ignition phase — Transcendence.

"So, as those who have been chosen of God, holy and beloved, put on a heart of compassion, kindness, humility, gentleness and patience." — Colossians 3:12

... are you ready?

IGNITION PHASE III
TRANSCENDENCE

MIRACLES

"Miracles are not contrary to nature but only contrary to what we know about nature." — St Augustine

You are already in the third major stage of awareness and self-work. Congratulations. You have already discovered some essential truths about our existence and your own nature and mission, by retreating from materialism and bringing yourself closer to our Creator. You have listened to my story and the stories of people I know, just to confirm what you already knew with your heart. You didn't do much more than looking inside for the truth and attuning your own inner compass which hardly ever lies to you, as you have discovered.

You know very well at this point that materialistic mainstream science cannot explain everything. Your attitude towards it must have changed drastically. You might see it as a demanding spoiled kid that wants everything RIGHT NOW and is used to getting things on a plate — instead of working in humility, patience and open heart to receive and appreciate the real truth. You might see mainstream science as a condescending or hypocritical institution that opposes religion but fails to see how religious it has become over the years and even centuries. At the same time, science refuses to even mention or acknowledge what real faith is.

"The day science begins to study non-physical phenomena, it will make more progress in one decade than in all the previous centuries of its existence." — Nikola Tesla

This is why I like to distinguish between mainstream science and real science; just as I can see the huge gap between mainstream religion and real faith. Both real science and real faith are pure and untainted by unnecessary rituals and blind beliefs, but they resonate with our intuition tremendously and awaken something inside us that excites us and reminds us of a forgotten knowledge. Both feel like precious treasures that we refuse to let go of, once we've discovered them after years of seeking.

Most importantly of all, real science and real faith work together, hand in hand. They do not oppose each other, they complement each other. They represent the combined enthusiasm, unyielding inner wisdom of seeking humans, and their motivation to excel in answering the questions posed by none other than our Creator. Only real science and real faith combined offer us the full picture, which works together with our own 360 vision that we've already discussed.

By trusting God and forming our science around Him and in His name, we are given 100% of the knowledge that we need for this stage of existence.

However, if we oppose God and still want to gain knowledge egotistically — and if we form our science around limited human perception and limitless human needs — our rebellion is met with gaining knowledge, yes; but this kind of knowledge comes from the dark places, that like to rebel to God too. If we exclude God from the picture, we negate him as the Source of light, and our channels become dark, whether it is apparent to us or not.

Even if our deeds are entirely motivated by the improvement of humanity, and our intentions to make human life better are pure in their essence, we are still missing the point. If we do everything in the name of mankind, and in the name of science, this is still not in the name of God. This leads to egocentrism which pushes away the knowledge of our Creator in a forceful and unnatural manner.

"Whatever you do, work at it with all your heart, as working for the Lord, not for human masters." — Colossians 3:23

Additionally, when we cherish the creation more than the Creator, we blind ourselves to the truth and we become intoxicated by materialism. In opposition to our purest intentions, come the dark messages from our unconscious which dictate our conscious actions and lead us to disgrace. We have already discussed how important it is to be wary of dark messages and spot them while they are still quiet hisses from the shadows.

When we ignore our biggest virtue amongst all — the awareness of our Heavenly Father — a lot of other real and natural things become invisible too, distant or unbelievable to us, because we've intentionally lost them in time. One of those things is miracles.

Miracles are very natural. They are gifts from the Source in return for the strong faith we harbour and the awareness we have worked to achieve and continue to achieve. Miracles are like colourful precious stones with a variety of forms and sizes — some are small but with very heart-warming shades, others are big, blue and mesmerising — almost alien. No matter what shade or size, when they come into your life, they bring you absolute happiness, relief or that thrilling feeling that everything is possible and that you're strong enough to endure everything now.

The more you are in this state, the more miracles come

into your life, and the bigger they are. This is why it is important to see most things as already manifested miracles. Surely, you have heard this quote by Einstein:

"There are only two ways to live your life. One is as though nothing is a miracle. The other is as though everything is a miracle."

There is indeed great wisdom in that. If we look at our lives as a series of moments, or scenes, or choices, we could see how that wise mindset does great wonders for us. Our lives are almost like the frames of a movie — we skip from one moment to another, and everything feels like a flow, but it is actually segregated. What we really have is only this exact instance, here and now. And we should cherish it. We should see it as a miracle, as a wonder.

Think about how worse it may have been. You could have been on the verge of despair or death right now. But you are not, you are so far away from the bottom. And this is a miracle on its own. Don't be afraid to juxtapose the polarities, and reflect on where you stand at this very moment. Think of it as a scale or a palette — even if you are in the mid-shades at present, you have just this much to do, in order to get to the brighter shades and receive your miracle.

And I promise you, if you stay long enough in the brighter shades, and preserve the mindset of thankfulness and endurance, you will receive your miracles so frequently that they will become an inseparable part of you. A shining fragment of your very own personality; and people will wonder at that. You will have a collection of those gemstones that will put that special sparkle in your eyes, and that magical frequency in your voice. They will also make you even happier and more self-aware, and definitely more fascinating as a person. Additionally, when you have already reached the top time and time again, you will come to a point where you are no longer able to fall under a certain dark shade. Everything for you will be from the mid-shades up, no matter what happens to you.

Your miracles will become bigger and brighter every time, and although they will start to feel very natural for you, you should never let go of your humility and gratitude. They are gifts after all; and along with the growth of your miracles, your faith should grow too. Never forget where you came from and how much help you've received on the way. Your awareness must increase with every wonder you achieve, and you must take the time to process it in quiet thankfulness, introspection and prayer. This must also feel natural to you at this point.

Last but not least, don't forget that miracles are very subjective and are something to cherish on a very personal and intimate level. A precious stone for you might seem like cheap junk for someone else who doesn't have your values or awareness. Your miracles resonate with your own personal intuition because in a way they are the product of it; they are the treasures you ultimately stumble upon by following this unique path of your intuition. With their polished bright surface, your miracles reflect nothing but your own deepest dreams and desires.

"Never surrender your hopes and dreams to the fateful limitations others have placed on their own lives. The vision of your true destiny does not reside within the blinkered outlook of the naysayers and the doom prophets. Judge not by their words, but accept advice based on the evidence of actual results. Do not be surprised should you find a complete absence of anything mystical or miraculous in the manifested reality of those who are so eager to advise you. Friends and family who suffer the lack of abundance, joy, love, fulfilment and prosperity in their own lives really have no business imposing their self-limiting beliefs on your reality experience." — Anthon St Maarten

***

I've had my own set of small and big miracles on the way, each very special and precious to me. The biggest one, as you already know, is finding my soulmate. It's a pure miracle that my thumb didn't get a spasm or something when I was swiping right on him on Tinder! We often joke about that. Can you imagine how much our lives would have changed if one of us just made a mistake, or got distracted and never saw the other one's profile? We would have probably met in another way, because of this unimaginably strong unconscious pull that we felt to one another. But it may have been in a more difficult time, or under the wrong circumstances.

People call that "fate", but I think this mindset is lazy and lacks full awareness. I believe that the special awakening that each of us ignited inside before we met easily led us to a huge mutual miracle that we shared in warm surprise and bliss. Surely, there is a plan for all of us — confused with the concept of "fate" — but you have to work in humility and awareness towards that plan; it doesn't come readily served for you.

I will also share with you one of my smaller miracles that ultimately led to something big for me — so that you can get the idea of how miracles work in reality and how to put them into practice. I hope that you will be able to follow through how they also pile up in time and how you have to be patient, resilient and enthusiastic, and to just keep going; ultimately, they lead you to greater and greater treasures along the way. This almost reminds me of the famous saying, "Follow the breadcrumbs to your success." Small steps lead to something big, more doors open before you, and you find more and more gems hidden at the most unexpected places.

You can never fail if you feel like Alice in Wonderland at all times. Everything seems interesting to you, a peculiar fairy tale that was created for you, and by you, with all its colours, all the possibilities, all the characters you meet on the way. You feel your own transition inside, and you transcend into a beautiful being, almost like a butterfly ready to spread its floral wings and fly away in freedom. Everything feels like a miracle, a precious stone, or a gift of wonder, if you open your mind and senses to the light that already flows within you.

When I officially moved to Plovdiv with my soulmate, after spending a wondrous summer together at the Bulgarian seaside, I wanted to settle down a bit, and do something big for my passions and professional development. Signing up for my second Master's, this time in psychology, was a no-brainer. Psychology was so satisfying and fulfilling to explore in depth, and later opened some great doors for me. But I had to work as well, and up to this point I had done just some bits and pieces here and there, just for the sake of saving money. Now I wanted to find my steady professional path on which I could use my potential, talents and qualifications to the fullest in order to help people and be fulfilled in my mission.

And so I started searching for jobs in Plovdiv. My intuition was guiding me in one particular direction which was unexpected for me, but I felt excited and intrigued regardless. I applied for many jobs in Human Resources. I knew nothing about Human Resources, just a general concept that it has something to do with interviewing people for jobs and supporting the managers and the office teams. But even knowing this much, it felt right at the time, and I was excited to apply for that.

Moreover, I found it quite interesting that some adverts said that the hiring managers would also consider people who have majored in linguistics and/or psychology. These were exactly my two specialties and my two major passions! I didn't think that it was by chance and kept applying even though I had no experience in HR which was listed as a main requirement, and also no idea what this business field fully meant.

Nothing. After weeks of applying — nothing. And you must already know by now that I am a person of action and doing nothing is not part of my nature. So I continued to apply a bit more broadly, just to have some alternatives. I was invited for an interview for a technical translator from English to Bulgarian. And for another interview for a customer support representative at an international call centre based in Plovdiv. Both seemed a bit boring, neither resonating fully with my inner Voice. They had some common points with my visualisation of a fulfilling office job within a cooperative team, but just weren't right on point. I still wanted to be safe and have different opportunities to choose from.

My interview for the translator job went successfully. But it was also eye-opening because I was perceptive of all the unexpected cues I got from it. The office was based on the top floor of an old renovated building in Plovdiv, and had that renaissance atmosphere which felt cosy and almost like home with its characteristic pinkish wallpapers, vintage fine decorations and warm wood furniture. However, it also felt separated from the real world somehow, as if you enter another era or another mindset when you go into the office. A mindset of cosy stagnation, calm reiteration of the same activities, and a peculiar stillness which felt warm, safe and secure, but also a bit frustrating.

It almost felt as if time somehow managed to stand still in this office, along with the people in it, as life was thriving and buzzing outside. It felt close to surreal when I saw the translators captured in there as if inside a frame of an old painting, inside their very safe and very introverted space of work. Their comfort zone felt so warm, idle and enclosed that I felt smothered and was lacking breath, even though it was a rather spacious office — and it wasn't that hot inside. The whole setting was surprising to me, as I had envisioned something very different.

The manager was a highly educated and eloquent woman in her late fifties who obviously had a very stable business niche in bilingual tech translation. We had a very calm and polite conversation at first which made me feel a bit drowsy; and then she gave me a couple of tech translation tasks which I did well, and she was pleased. She gave me more time than I needed, though. I couldn't help but feel a bit bored with the task, and I already couldn't see myself engaged in this activity for the majority of my time. I had done tons of translation-related tasks in my university studies, but they were more creative and predominantly related to fictional literature.

"There is a need for all types of translators," I thought to myself, "and this is the current demand, so I should adapt to it."

The manager then introduced me to the team of

translators, around eleven or twelve, who were all nice-looking young people my age, in their mid-twenties or a bit older. All of them wore shirts, part of their business attire, but their sweaters on top revealed their partiality for cosiness and feeling at home even at their workplace. I found that endearing and interesting. Most of them wore glasses and were a bit more stooped than they should be for their age. They appeared very introverted as well, understandably. I thought about how I would give in to my own introverted nature and fall hard into my comfort zone, if I joined this team.

What made the biggest impression on me, however, was that they didn't smile at all, even though they were trying to be friendly. It was nothing against me and I would never take it personally; in fact, I already had a theory why they were like this, and couldn't help but empathise with them, even though nobody asked me to, and I felt stupid for that. I sensed that they were inside some deep slumber in the way they communicated and had difficulties sharing important stuff about their job. They seemed bored with it but had probably never actually questioned why they were doing it if it was so boring.

It's never the job that's boring, it's the lack of meaning you put into your activities.

Naturally, I met them with my characteristic smile and enthusiasm, and asked them questions about what they loved about their job, aiming for the positive side of things as always. This was the whole idea of the manager when she allowed me to meet her employees, while she remained in her separate office. However, I noticed that my positive questioning resembled more and more an interview process which made the translators more alert from this change in the environment.

I thought that there must hardly be any changes or surprises in this office that would wake them up from their slumber; and I also got the sense that no one there had asked the question "Why?" ever. But that's why I was there and wanted to try and help after all, even if I may have appeared as an insolent intruder.

And so I asked one of the girls, who had been working there for three years already, the ultimate interview question: "So what are your true reasons behind choosing this job?" She paused; her eyes fluttered for a second. There was obviously movement in there, and I was beginning to have hopes that I would get some meaning from this whole situation after all. But to my instant disappointment, she answered: "Well, we are all linguists here. What else can we do?"

This answer caused a burning sensation in me. What else can we do? I've had an implosion of images in me about those young people and their lives, choices, experiences and prospects for the future. She spoke on behalf of all of them, as if they were all trapped inside a small dark chamber together in their idleness and lack of motivation, and she was their spokesperson. I felt deep compassion for all of them, but also the nudge to say something to wake them up from the way they categorised themselves, and how they enclosed their potential inside a small box.

It's wonderful to be a translator! It's enough to be a translator! It's a very noble profession! But you have to follow your path of meanings until you get there and become one. You have to be awake and in tune with your inner callings. Is this really your mission in life? Trust your intuition! If it is, then do it with love, enthusiasm, smiles and meaning! Be a translator and develop your skills, passions and qualities as a translator. Do it not because you made the absent-minded choice to study linguistics in the past, and this is your only way to go now, but because you love it and you want to be the best at it!

"Each man had only one genuine vocation — to find the way to himself ... His task was to discover his own destiny — not an arbitrary one — and to live it out wholly and resolutely within himself. Everything else was only a would-be existence, an attempt at evasion, a flight back to the ideals of the masses, conformity and fear of one's own inwardness."
— Hermann Hesse

I couldn't say those words out loud as it would be extremely impolite and awkward, but they got stuck inside my mind for long afterwards. I said something along the lines that "everyone has their callings for what they should do professionally, and I just thought that this was your passion". No reaction whatsoever. So much for my search for meaning and reason. I guess it was just me and my insolent questionings again... I felt awkward but confident in my stance.

I took a lot of cues and symbols from this interview, as my outer and inner senses were sharp and perceptive — and honestly, I wanted them to remain this way even in the professional world. For this exact reason, I thought that when I received the offer, I would most probably reject it unless nothing else came up my way. Or if the thing that came up was actually somehow worse for my own mission and vision. I introspected back then, and it didn't take me long to confirm with myself that my path of meanings didn't lead me to the translator profession, even though I was a linguistics graduate just like them. I just hoped that they would find their meanings in what they did and be happy with it; especially taking into account the noble and respected profession that they had.

But it was just not for me; I wanted something different. I knew that in theory, there was just not much I could choose from, being a linguistics graduate who was currently in the midst of psychological studies. But this was only in theory. I knew that the right thing would practically come my way destroying all odds, and I felt a warm and exciting anticipation. I had faith. I was unyielding to my dreams and found myself remaining firmly in the bright-shaded mindset — the mindset in which miracles happen.

I visualised my dream job a lot. I wanted to find meaning in my profession every single day, I wanted to know exactly why I am doing this or that activity. I wanted to ask questions, but also to give answers. The idea of interviewing people became more and more appealing. I wanted to expand my theoretical and abstract wisdom with practical applications and knowledge about how real industries work. I wanted to find connections and solve problems. I wanted to plan and organise, and then execute the plans in my own way.

I wanted to help people achieve something, find something, connect with other people with the same interests or passions. I wanted to analyse people, and write about their characters, so that other people would learn about them and connect with them. I wanted to be an intermediary; and a consultant-level specialist in my field. I wanted other people to depend on me and my professionalism, because I knew that I wouldn't let them down. I wanted to express my acquired knowledge creatively, in writing, speaking and advertising, with the mere reason to help and assist people in their passions and professions.

Just as I was beginning to connect the dots and realise

more clearly that what I was looking for was precisely and unequivocally HR, I went to that other interview — for the customer support representative.

This office was huge, at least two hundred people were working there, and everything was new and modern, in that minimalistic cold tech style, with white, grey and blue as predominant colours. It was situated on the sixth floor of a newly constructed large building, in one of the biggest districts of Plovdiv. I later found out that the company was part of a huge international corporation with call centre sites all over the world, only one of them being in Plovdiv.

Unlike the translators' office, this one had a particular buzz and even stress to it — all the young people were moving around feverishly, always in a hurry. I noticed that they used chip cards with sensors to go inside and outside the building, which probably reported the exact times they took for their breaks. This was probably why I noticed upon entering that there were some young people in groups who smoked very fast and put out their cigarettes in half, only to hurry back inside while telling loud jokes and masking their anxiety and hurriedness. Still, I thought that this could be my imagination at this point.

My interview was with a young male team leader, not much older than myself but already with a whole team of twenty people just under his supervision. Strict business attire, white shirt and blue suit; I found it rather ironic, given that the predominant colours in the whole building were exactly the same. When I had the thought that he did that on purpose because this was actually camouflage, I almost laughed inappropriately. I knew that I was underdressed for this interview, but I wasn't too concerned about it because I knew that everything was an unnecessary ego display when it came to those expensive suits and watches. However, I sensed that he worked very hard, and his suit wasn't just a glossy cover.

He was very strict and formal in his communication as well; spoke too fast, shot so many questions one after the other about my studies, qualifications and experience that I had to adapt to his pace and attitude. I did it unproblematically, but he still made me feel nervous and alert, not giving me a second to take a breath. I remember how I thought back then that I would do a much better job if I were the interviewer. And then felt bad that I was thinking this; this distracted me a bit from the present moment and I asked him to repeat his last question. But in the end, I did OK on the interview.

He gave me a task later which was actually a test for my English level — since I was going to work only with English-speaking customers. Unfortunately, he told me nothing about the job, he didn't let me meet the team or at least see the workplace in which my whole days would pass, with a headset and with a complex database to use. Nothing practical, which left me confused. But then again, he had given me an easy to mid-level test in English. English was pretty much the only thing I knew how to do in this job, and he was testing me on it.

"That's how they do it, and they must know better," I thought. "They're far more experienced than I am, even though I still don't know exactly what they're doing."

When I finished, he just walked me out with what seemed like a forced smile and the words, "Thank you, we will be in touch shortly if you were successful."

On my way home, I felt nothing short of confusion and anxiety. I had more questions now about this job and workplace than before I entered the building. What I knew was that if I chose this job, I would be just another brick in the wall, just another insignificant pawn in the game of the big corporate kings whom I would never meet or reach in any way. Not because I couldn't, but because I wouldn't. Reaching the top of the corporate ladder in the conventional sense has never appealed to me. There are just so many, many wrong things with it. You have to be greatly awakened but also ready to give out your whole life and time, in order to survive in the corporate jungle, and truly make a difference.

I knew I could endure all of that; it wasn't that much. But was it worth it? Was it part of my mission? Would I truly make a difference with this job? I was confused and already a bit overwhelmed with this job search I had a couple more phone interviews for other office jobs that seemed more and more irrelevant to my visions of what I wanted to do.

I applied to one more HR job which made a huge impression on me. The advert was very neat and grammatically correct, very well structured and professional but also written in a friendly and welcoming way. It resembled the way I would write it, I thought. The logo and the name of the company were quite cool as well, which always held great importance in my mind of ideas, colours, symbols and meanings.

Another two weeks passed and while I was still in the bright mindset, expectant for the best, I had no calls for any of the HR jobs. I had received the two offers from the translation office and the customer support centre, and I had to decide fast. They had both given me a notice of one week to decide, and this week was passing too quickly. I really needed the job to support my psychological studies at this point, as the majority of our savings with my partner from our summer jobs were already spent on repairs and purchases for our new home in Plovdiv. So I had no other choice, but to decide between the two offers — take the lesser evil, I thought.

I knew I was disregarding my intuition. It was the Sunday of this fateful week, and I was reluctantly writing an email to the manager of the translation office that I was accepting the job offer, and would like to start on the following Wednesday… when I received the long-awaited call, against all odds…

***

It was a miracle — finally someone contacting me for an HR job! A younger woman, possibly in her late thirties or early forties from the sound of it, with a very soft and friendly voice. She apologised that she contacted me so late on Sunday, but she had been travelling and couldn't phone me earlier. When I asked about the name of the company, it turned out that it was that last HR job I applied for, with the awesome logo and advert! I was so intrigued and excited but wanted to sound cool on the phone. I couldn't believe that she was phoning me out of nowhere, on Sunday and just as I was accepting the other offer.

That right there was the miracle at play. A small gem, but an important one, as it would lead me to bigger treasures later on in my life.

She was the first one to walk me through everything about the job and what was going to be expected from me as a recruiter; how my qualifications and skills would fit greatly into her small but ambitious company, and her vision. She described the office, the location, the types of clients they had, and she made me imagine myself right there. She had studied my CV thoroughly and when she actually asked me questions, they were right on point, very relevant, and I felt very confident answering them. She also sounded extremely down to earth, although I knew that she was an ambitious and successful businesswoman; we would actually share jokes, which was a very refreshing thing for me given the slightly inadequate interviews I had before that.

Everything that she told me sounded right for me — from the salary and the location (it turned out the workplace was just a couple of blocks away from our home in Plovdiv!) to the bigger things, the meaning of the role; its purpose of helping people find their perfect job and connecting them with seeking employers who would be our clients — being the intermediary between the two sides, and the consultant which I had dreamed to become.

I would write a commentary about each candidate I interview, describing their character, demeanour and suitability for the job, and pass it on to the employer to see. It was so interesting and so close to what I had been imagining. And I would receive so much information about it; nothing was hidden or confusing — all the new information was extremely clear and available for me.

And then I realised something. I couldn't help but ask the manager why she chose me if I didn't have experience in HR and recruitment. She laughed quietly and said:

"The job requires excellent levels of Bulgarian and English literacy, great communication skills and knowledge of people — and this is what I am looking for; everything else can be learned. I am ready to train you on that. Besides, even though I've had many great candidates with experience, I am just following my intuition here and you seem to be one of the strongest candidates out of the CVs, even with the obvious disadvantage."

I couldn't believe that she said that; it may have been just two or three sentences, but they gave me so much more information about the nature of the job, how my training would unwind, and also what her character is. I knew that she was an intuitive type and by assessing her intelligence, style of communication and sense of humour, I knew that she would be a great mentor and a friend. I couldn't hold my excitement and enthusiasm any longer. I almost shouted over the phone when I said, "I'm taking the job!"

She was obviously pleasantly surprised that everything happened so smoothly and quickly. She laughed cheerfully again, and said, "OK, I am glad to hear that — just meet me on Wednesday at ten, so that we can prepare your contract and you can see your working place. You won't have any colleagues to meet, because so far, I am the only person dealing with recruitment, but you will meet my ladies from the payroll department. You can feel free to start on the same day, or the day after!"

And just like that... without an official interview, just after a single phone call, I got my dream job that I had no experience in. The best manager I could ask for phoned me at her last chance on Sunday, sensing the urgency, and following the path of her intuition which had crossed paths with my own intuition.

This is how small miracles work. And you should embrace them and be thankful for them. A lot of people would say that it's a perfect coincidence, momentary chance, part of probability theory, or anything that makes it seem chaotic and unplanned. But the truth is that this was just another major proof in my life that there is indeed a plan designed for me, and it gets confirmed and reconfirmed by my intuition.

The next two years on this job were a delight. The office felt like home to me with its warm orange colours, new furniture, stylish paintings and modern but cosy atmosphere. I learned so much, I did so much, I helped so much. I was a "natural", as my boss would say on frequent occasions. As I gained more and more confidence, I would have more placements of people on jobs, and our business would stabilise and grow. This is why we had to recruit and hire several more recruiters at a time to take a load off my work, a highly fulfilling task on its own. I was a young woman still in my mid-twenties, but I was highly respected in the field even by high-level managers, well established in the industries long before I had even been in middle school. They were dependent on me for recruiting the best specialists to join their team and make a difference. It was unbelievable, but it was real.

A lot of small shiny miracles didn't fail to take place for me on a daily basis — I got that continuous feeling of being in the right place, at the right time, doing the right thing. I got a lot of small and big pushes from the Source, with just the connections or the piece of knowledge that I needed at each step of my progression. I acknowledged them all. My job was very fast paced and demanding, but so satisfying, so interesting and different every day that I would go home tired but fulfilled, with a smile on my face. My enthusiasm, hope and faith, never ever failed me.

We got more and more clients, each more interesting and better paid than the other. Our business was just doing great even though it started just with me as the sole recruiter in the department. Just after the first year, I had already become very good friends with my boss, and we somehow felt and communicated as equals. We would go on business trips together, on conferences and training together, on important meetings negotiating together as associates. We would talk openly about anything; nothing was left behind or unclear, even personal stuff. We had built this mutual trust so easily, so naturally and intuitively that it enriched the purpose of the business in no time, which was ultimately to make profit by helping people.

I was promoted twice in those two years, and my manager was planning a third promotion. She had another separate business as well and was truly considering making me an associate and giving out her whole recruitment business for me to manage and develop — just the way I felt was right. Our department already consisted of three other recruiters apart from me. I had all the freedom and respect in this position, in this company, with this manager. I was so full of thankfulness that I would cast rays of gratitude and happiness to everyone and everything; I knew that I was making people happier just by communicating with them, even if it was regarding their professions or businesses.

I felt the magic of my transcendence at that stage of my existence. Miracles had become an unseparated part of my own personality, and people kept wondering at how I was doing this or that. They kept asking me what my secret was. I was glad that it had become so obvious at this point that I was an unyielding believer, and this could be seen in nothing else but my actions. I never preached, or even talked about God, which was probably a mistake on my part. I guess I didn't want to be intrusive to people with my "beliefs". Still, people would clearly see that I was doing something right by the way I lived my life and came to me for advice. At this point I was wielding the "law of attraction" quite skilfully, like a familiar weapon with which I was very used to, and it was doing wonders for me. I stumbled upon more and more precious little gems on my way up and received them in bright gratitude.

I majored in psychology successfully, again on top of my class and had attracted some attention without trying. I was invited to a Norwegian university to participate in a very interesting research project that had always been a major passion of mine in psychology. I spent several wonderful months in Norway, meeting new kindred souls. I explored the Scandinavian lands as well and added even more magical moments to my already rich library of memories. In my university work, I got a sense of what psychologists in academic settings do. It was interesting and important, but honestly the most exciting part for me was recruiting and interviewing the participants for my qualitative research tests.

Moreover, when I returned to Bulgaria the lead psychology professor at the Plovdiv University reached me and offered me a PhD position. I was very pleasantly surprised and thankful, especially because I knew that PhD is not offered to everyone; people usually apply for it and go through a very competitive process of selection. I was interested and considered it for a while, but I was just too passionate about Human Resources to change my path at this point. I actually considered continuing working at my firm, no matter if I got the associate HR Manager position or not. But just then I received another offer which combined everything that I was good at, and everything that I had worked hard for.

The offer was just too good to refuse, and I could hardly believe that it even existed as an option. Following the small miracle gems on my path had led me to a bigger treasure. All it took me to receive this gift was to sharpen my senses and be patient and interactive with the changes in my environment, and all the small miracles that inevitably came in my way.

They offered me a Recruitment Consultant job, based in beautiful Prague, for an international company with many recruitment markets and a lot to choose from. Excitingly enough, they had matched me for the psychology and therapy markets across the United Kingdom. I would connect psychologists and therapists with their ideal workplace and employer. This couldn't be more relevant. I already had two years of very successful experience in HR, I had studied English linguistics, culture and geography, and also psychology and how it applies in clinical and academic settings. I was chosen to be a recruiter and a professional career consultant, at an upgraded job tailored to my ultimate interests.

As much as I respected my Bulgarian manager and appreciated everything, she'd done for me, I felt that I'd be right to say yes to that new international offer. It was a difficult decision and it felt like betrayal; after all, this wasn't just a job for me, it had become my space, my second home and my small path of success — and my manager had become my very own teacher and friend. But it was time for me to try something new and develop my skills on an international level, and she understood that completely, which relieved my guilt a bit.

The best thing was that I left her business with positivity and with many great plans for the future. Before I left, we hired two new employees in my place whom I trained thoroughly and prepared for the next steps. My previous manager's business is thriving now, thanks to her professionalism, kindness, adaptability and uncompromising intuition. I could never thank her enough for the flying start she gifted me with, in my dream profession. We naturally stayed friends afterwards — important relationships of shared trust, warmth and respect should never be abandoned.

***

And so, I took the new offer. Together with my soulmate, we planned together, and we organised everything systematically. It was a huge step, but we did it. He managed to get a great job in 3D graphic design and CGI too, we found a cosy rent apartment in the heart of Prague, and we settled here. I am writing this book in Prague, right here and now — feeling more inspired and enthusiastic than ever.

My work is going great, it's more interesting than everything I've done so far, and more fulfilling than I ever imagined. During the intensive recruitment training, I managed to step up even more and learn the finer details of the business. Who knows what the future holds; but at this point I have zero fear or anxiety even if there are obstacles from time to time. My faith has proven to work out greatly, and in the end, I am always a winner thanks to the Source; I always end up helping people just the way I was designed to help people. And I can no longer fall under a certain dark shade of living.

Going back in time and following the thread of my greatest passion and profession, I can't help but wonder at the initial small gems that were given to me by the Source. Everything from my decision to study psychology and my sudden interest in HR, and that first call of my Bulgarian manager up until this point — was so organised, so well put in time that I couldn't ask for a better and smoother turn of events. The key thing was that I was always aware — at every step of progression; at every daily struggle or failure; at every moment I stumbled and fell but decided to stand up again. I was always awake and chose not to ignore a single sign or synchronicity along my path.

God always gives signs; people just choose to ignore them. I decided to take them all in and be in control at all times. Not all stages of planning and organisation were easy either — some took time, energy and resilience. But I just kept going. We just kept going — as a super couple that managed to ignite our common power flame and face everything that life would bring us.

Throughout my professional path, I knew I was always doing the right thing, according to God's unique design for me. I was born with a free will like every human being, but with that free will I decided to walk on His path, rather than be led astray from it. And people could see this as well, just in my example, in the way I have been living my life — nothing more, nothing less. Most importantly, I learned many important lessons from this whole journey, one of the most essential ones being patience. I have a lot more to learn too.

I know that it will get even better now, since He also gave me the inspiration and energy to write this book, even though I am extremely busy at work; so that I can share my modest but special example and acquired wisdom, in the humblest intention to inspire and help more people. Even one person would be enough, in order for my creative energy to make sense and be worth it.

Be that one person. That special person.

I invite you freely to this journey of transcendence — which is ultimately your last portal in this physical existence. Who knows where it leads you after you go through it; I don't know, as I am at this stage as well. Perhaps miracles of grander scale will take place, and maybe the whole of humanity will gradually be affected by this new vision. Perhaps hidden knowledge will be far more easily accessible and visible to us than before; and this additional vague sense which I call intuition will become as strong as our very eyesight. Possibly, people will finally take a more humane and compassionate approach, and people on a mass scale will finally take a peek on the inside. Perhaps the channel of light will be our only source of energy on this physical plane, just as Tesla envisioned. Only God knows... and I am sure that everything is already mapped out in His Great plan for us. Choose His plan with your free will too, and you will never be mistaken.

Having let go of your ego, you paradoxically become the most appreciated and respected version of yourself — in your work, in your relationships, in your interaction with your Inner self. Being vulnerable, authentic and uncompromisingly kind ultimately makes you unimaginably strong. The way your light reserve grows bigger every time you give out light freely may sound nonsensical, but as you have discovered, it actually makes more sense than anything else. And that is the biggest treasure of them all, the most precious gift which you meet with your awareness, continuous humility and patient motivation to help.

This is your transcendence.

And I promise you: a lot more magical things besides miracles become natural to you in this higher state.

SYNCHRONICITIES

"I do believe in an everyday sort of magic — the inexplicable connectedness we sometimes experience with places, people, works of art and the like; the eerie appropriateness of moments of synchronicity; the whispered voice, the hidden presence, when we think we're alone." — Charles de Lint

I decided to read a bit more about synchronicities before writing about them in my book. The mystical description I saw on the first page of Wikipedia made total sense to me and was rather intriguing, and I wasn't surprised at all to see the exact opposite stance of mainstream science a bit later on in the text.

Synchronicity (German: *Synchronizität*) is a concept, first introduced by analytical psychologist Carl Jung, which holds that events are "meaningful coincidences" if they occur with no causal relationship yet seem to be meaningfully related. During his career, Jung furnished several different definitions of it. Jung defined synchronicity as an "acausal connecting (togetherness) principle", "meaningful coincidence", "acausal parallelism" or "meaningful coincidence of two or more events where something other than the probability of chance is involved". (Wikipedia)

Jung has always expressed himself secretively and with a certain pinch of mysticism, part of which I appreciate his profound work so much. There is indeed something other than the probability of chance involved; and it's very simple. It's the presence of God — and his plan for you. Even when something seems like a coincidence or a game of chances, it's not — it's related to the Greater good with a tiny but nonetheless existent thread. We cannot see the threads, with the exception of some especially gifted people — I could think of at least five phenomenal Bulgarian psychics who lived in the last 150 years that could see those threads along with many other things. But the majority of us don't necessarily see the connections. We feel them.

And that's enough — that's absolutely sufficient for this reality, as long as you don't intentionally suppress that feeling or completely reject it. Just like mainstream science did:

"Synchronicity is considered pseudoscience because it is neither testable nor falsifiable. Mainstream science explains synchronicities as mere coincidences or spurious correlations which can be described by laws of statistics (for instance, by the law of truly large numbers) and confirmation biases." (Wikipedia).

We can't test everything to prove it or falsify it; just as we cannot always use our five senses to test reality. Science itself has admitted how limited our five-sense perception is, and yet we continue to hypocritically use these outworn instruments to try and explain something so deep, so otherworldly. Of course, they would deem synchronicity as "pseudo-science"; it's far more convenient this way. Just as it is always convenient to hide behind those "large numbers" in order to adjust their limited theories to our reality. In this regard, when mainstream science even mentions "confirmation bias", it is highly hypocritical.

Besides, their conveniently designed "Law of large numbers" is the statistical theory to go to for everything. You can't explain an extra-sensory phenomenon — large numbers.

You can't explain a heart-warming and eye-opening miracle — large numbers. "The law of truly large numbers (a statistical adage), states that with a large enough number of samples, any outrageous (i.e., unlikely in any single sample) thing is likely to be observed."

In other words, this is a very convenient way to exclude our Creator and His contribution from the picture. So when they face a gap like synchronicity or people who can see things that are outside the physical, they explain all of that with truly large numbers, or truly large spaces. It's almost humorous; but understandable — after all scientists are just humans, like all of us.

"Even a scientist is a human being. So it is natural for him, like others, to hate the things he cannot explain. It is a common illusion to believe that what we know today is all we ever can know. Nothing is more vulnerable than scientific theory, which is an ephemeral attempt to explain facts and not an everlasting truth in itself." — C.G. Jung.

Besides, they are obviously struggling to connect the dots but sadly, their ego is rarely tamed down enough to admit that. One famous and friendly-looking mainstream physicist Michio Kaku admitted it once, and I doubt that enough people took notice of what he said:

"There is a crisis in cosmology. Usually in science when we're off by a factor of two or a factor of ten, we call that hope — we say something's wrong with the theory. However, in cosmology we're off by a factor of 10^{120}! That is one with a hundred and twenty zeros! This is the largest mismatch between theory and experiment in the history of science."

This goes to show how far off the mainstream scientific method could be. And even though this is an extreme example, it clearly sums up how hypocritical and blind modern science could be in its general beliefs. Mainstream science also readily trusts something that cannot be proven or disproven with the five senses, similarly to religion; however, it disregards that real faith can be felt with the heart: with the inner senses of the soul. Surely, since they cannot be physically seen, they do not exist for mainstream science either. They are "pseudo-science" at best. Do you see where the limits lie?

"Your assumptions are your windows on the world. Scrub them off every once in a while, or the light won't come in." — Isaac Asimov.

You see, it is not that difficult to admit that there is something that you don't know, or that you don't have the slightest idea how to reach a certain truth. But the problem lies in the unwillingness to let go of ego, and finally receive the real answers from within, and without much testing. Of course, some things can be tested and should be tested, but other things cannot be grasped in the slightest by mainstream science, because it is just a fraction of the Greater truth's framework. It takes humility and quiet profound introspection to admit that. It takes spiritual growth to realise that there is actually something bigger than you, and this thing is not the lifeless "cosmos". It takes an open mind and heart to embrace the truth of a Higher Power, of a divine living Creator who looks over you and gifts you with synchronicities and miracles.

The signs are actually very obvious and should be the main focus of science — there are patterns in our world; in nature; in our bodies and DNA, in our smallest particles' cells. The Golden ratio, Fibonacci numbers, the repetition of fractals. All these signs are mathematically proven to be perfect and carefully designed.

If there is a design, there is surely a Designer.

Mathematics is truly the language of God, as they say — it can be found everywhere on our physical plane, in the frequency of waves, in music, in colours, in all four elements: earth, water, air, fire. Some people are gifted to see the manifestation of this language, just like in the movie *A Beautiful Mind*. There is a mathematical value to every energy, and even if you can't see it, you can actually feel the change of frequency in the mood swings of a conversation, for example.

This is all part of his Great design, and you don't need to fully understand it or know absolutely everything about it, as fascinating as it is. You just need to know that it's there and you play a role in this dynamic and interactive system. It's far easier to admit that mainstream science has been missing one key element — the presence of God, and it would save them many, many, hardships and fruitless years of research (not to even mention how much money this would save them). It would be far easier than hiding behind those large numbers and spaces for sure, which are extremely counter-intuitive anyway. Unfortunately, however, it is human nature to rather listen to the fallen hisses from the dark and rebel against the Creator, rather than embrace His love and power. And mainstream science has become a great tool just for that.

The truth is that you will never be able to see all threads and explain all mathematical patterns. Some humans in history have been close — like Leonardo DaVinci, Fibonacci, Tesla, William Gann, and others. But they have also admitted using additional senses for their work and ingenious ideas; they have also admitted a certain presence of a Higher Power. Only in this way were they able to develop a strong sense for these golden laws and invisible threads, witness more synchronicities than the average person, and utilise them in creating something meaningful which inevitably remained in history.

"Synchronicity occurs at the intersection of your awareness, response, perspective, and action." — Andrea Goeglein.

Synchronicity is real. Synchronicity is something very common when you have reached the transcendence state — it is part of the miraculous nature of your faith and the confidence in your design. It's related to your awareness and ability to perceive signs of upcoming wonders.

I would go even further and state that synchronicities are those little signs or pointers on your road, which precede miracles or announce for upcoming important events. They are the arrows which you find all too often when you are indeed on the right path. Synchronicities must be taken in with contentment, awareness and calmness, and are nothing to be afraid of.

"There are only two symptoms of enlightenment, just two indications that a transformation is taking place within you toward a higher consciousness. The first symptom is that you stop worrying. Things don't bother you anymore. You become light-hearted and full of joy. The second symptom is that you encounter more and more meaningful coincidences in your life, more and more synchronicities. And this accelerates to the point where you actually experience the miraculous." — Deepak Chopra.

Synchronicities are highly subjective and tailored to a person's life and experiences. Just like with miracles, the signs that you see in the outer world may hold a great meaning to

168

you but would be nonsensical to someone else. The other people may not even see those signs, and this is key. Synchronicities make an impression on you because they are actually externalisations of your own unconscious mind. Those little signs that you see everywhere for a short period of time are instant manifestations of your deepest thoughts, desires, plans and expectations.

This is not confirmation bias, as you usually don't expect to see them at all. However, they attract your attention and appear more vivid than any other object, symbol or person surrounding them. They just stick out with their colours and meanings from the surrounding greyness, and you can't help it. It is a natural and intuitive process of reading the signs with your inner senses, as these are signs sent just for you to see. Don't start looking for them, as they come on their own.

Listening to your inner compass, you can easily distinguish which signs are true and which are not — judging by the immediacy and unexpectedness of their emergence, and the natural ignition of a specific feeling within your heart. They could also trigger an answer to a question, a slight scolding to a mistake you've made, a new creative idea, a flashback of something important you've forgotten, or a full imaginary chart of a plan that you've long postponed. It really depends on where your soul stands at the moment, and what is due to happen next. It's kind of exciting, when you think about it.

Considering it more deeply, synchronicities are flashes of events that belong to the spiritual world, which manifest in the physical world for a special observer to see. Don't forget that before the great events happen on our plane, they have already "happened" in the Deep. They are written, sketched, designed

— by our Creator and in accordance with the Greater good. Maybe not in too many details, but are nevertheless there, ready to uncoil like a film tape in our material reality.

Synchronicities are glimpses to these original sketches and come in the form of visual or sound imagery in our normal everyday lives. Exactly because everything is designed beforehand in the spiritual realm, there are some people gifted with more access to this original source of information. The greatest psychics and prophecy tellers can predict very specific events in the future with almost 100% accuracy for the same reason and according to this single law. We shall inspect that thoroughly in an upcoming chapter.

A very common synchronicity is to think of a person that you haven't seen in ages, and this person gives you a call or a text, or even shows up in front of you unexpectedly. Always look for your personal meaning for that. How is that person important for you? What part of your life does this person represent? Do you have unfinished business with them or with your previous life stage? Do you owe them something or do they owe you? (Could be time, attention, answers, it doesn't have to be money). Could this person be the bridge to another person, or to an important event for you? What key connections does this person have? And most importantly, how can you help this person?

Since he or she is an instant manifestation of something your intuition warned you about seconds ago, you have to take it into account and search for the meaning. More often than not, the person comes to you with a ready answer and this is why they decided to give you a call in the first place; but you can always just ask them generally and see what the reply would be.

Another synchronicity is to observe repetitive symbols or numbers in the external world and in your dreams. I am not a big fan of numerology; however, I do believe that the different numbers hold special personal meanings to the souls experiencing them. If mathematics is the language of our Creator, then the numbers should be the words of this language. It's all about how your subjective reservoir of unconscious imagery renders specific chunks of information to you in the outside world, in order to communicate with your conscious mind. Think about that time when you saw your special or favourite number everywhere, but you didn't make anything of it, although it made an impression on you. What does this number represent to you?

I've always loved the number 12; it holds a special meaning to me. I was born on the 12th date of the month, 12 is the number of the apostles of Christ, 12 hours in half a day, 12 months, 12 constellations and zodiac signs, etc. It's a very divine number and I've always seen it with the character of a wise and calm teacher, great organiser and leader. I've always imagined 12 as an end to a cycle, a whole finished circle.

For me, 12 is the number which has the full vision from above to everything that's taken place so far, it is the ripe and wise end of a journey, and the portal to a new beginning born out of it. I would see the number 12 repeatedly when I finally found my faith at the age of seventeen; I didn't know immediately what it meant but I remember feeling that it was somehow important. Thinking about it in retrospection after that, I realised that this was the end of one cycle to which I had full vision then, and a promise of a completely new one being born out of the ashes, like a phoenix.

"Every transformation demands as its precondition 'the ending of a world' — the collapse of an old philosophy of life."

171

— C.G. Jung, *Man and His Symbols.*

I would see 12 over and over again just before I found my soulmate too — and I already knew what it meant — another cycle in my life had just finished, and new promising events were upcoming. The synchronicities in my life have never failed me, as they have always been the predecessors of something important or big.

I think it is very key that I never look out for them, and they have always found me during an introspective or distracted moment of brooding. I am already used to taking them in a calm and appreciative state of awareness that they have come as messages from above — through my own unconscious channel of ideas and symbols. It's not by chance that exactly this or that symbol emerged from the Deep; it has to be connected with something right here and now, with my current soul progression and the challenges prepared for me. I almost want to say that there is nothing magical about synchronicities, as they come as a product of mere psychology and divine intervention, but that would be unappreciative as everything about them feels deeply magical.

I want you to think about your own special symbols and numbers. How often have you seen them externalised by mere "coincidence"? Think about a grapheme or a lexeme that attracted your attention on the newspaper of a man reading it in the public transport — and you couldn't get your eyes off that symbol. Why?

Think about graffiti, billboards, posters, banners, internet ads and suggested videos, repetitive old songs in your head or on the radio, the appearance of the same "random" person over and over again, you name it. There are no limits to where, how and in the face of whom you can get your signs. The way in which you receive them doesn't really matter. But have you followed the invisible threads and made the connections? This is the question you should be asking yourself.

It is vital to receive synchronicities with a clear and stable mind. I cannot overlook the fact that many people become delusional by actively looking for their signs in every nook and cranny or seeking a connection when there is none. This is why I can't stress enough on how essential it is to have divine awareness, on-point calibration of character, strong objectivity and a fair share of scepticism, in order to receive the signs in the proper way. In your transcendence state, you no longer have the frivolousness to falter or waver in a beginner's fashion. So be ever conscious of the perception of both your outer and inner senses. You already know that none of this is child's play, and you have to be fully aware at every step.

Synchronicities, as I mentioned, can also take the form of special signs and symbols appearing and reappearing in your dreams, not only in the external world. This actually makes them more powerful and meaningful, as there is no conscious control on our part when we dream. Our mind during sleep speaks the unconscious language of the Deep. We take in everything in its pure form; and what is left to do is just to interpret it.

For that reason, we need to pay special attention to the symbols in our dreams which are also highly subjective. Especially if we have reoccurring dreams, or dreams that partially or fully become reality after we've had them. Jung knew this very well, and that's why he integrated dream interpretation in his unique therapy sessions with clients and patients. Special symbols in dreams that later manifest in reality are synchronicities on steroids, and that is why I decided to devote a separate chapter just for them.

SYMBOLS AND DREAMS

"Thus, the interpretation of dreams, whether by the analyst or by the dreamer himself, is for the Jungian psychologist an entirely personal and individual business (and sometimes an experimental and very lengthy one as well) that can by no means be undertaken by rule of thumb. The converse of this is that the communications of the unconscious are of the highest importance to the dreamer — naturally so, since the unconscious is at least half of his total being — and frequently offer him advice or guidance that could be obtained from no other source." — C.G. Jung, *Man and His Symbols*

Jung had a very peculiar dream one night. He dreamed of a house that looked like his house but felt quite unfamiliar to him. The upper storey was detailed and known for him — furnished in modern Rococo style. However, he did not know what the lower floor looked like.

When he went downstairs to check, everything was much older; this part of the house looked as if it dated from the 15th or 16th century. The furnishings were mediaeval; the floors were made of a red brick. Jung went from one room to another, thinking how he really wanted to explore the whole house at this point.

He came upon a heavy door and opened it. A stone stairway led down into the cellar, descending once again. He found himself in a dark but beautiful vaulted place, which looked exceedingly ancient. The walls dated from Roman times; the floor was of stone slabs. On one of these slabs, Jung discovered a ring. The stone slab lifted, and he saw a staircase of narrow stone steps leading down, even further into darkness.

He descended once again and entered a low cave. There were scattered bones, dust and broken pottery; like remains of a primitive culture. He discovered two human skulls, obviously very old and half-disintegrated...

And then he woke up.

It was plain to him that the house represented a kind of an image of the psyche. Consciousness was represented by the salon — the upper storey. With its modern Rococo style, it had an inhabited atmosphere.

The ground floor with the mediaeval surroundings stood for the first level of the unconscious.

The deeper Jung went, the more alien and the darker the

scene became. The Roman cellar and the prehistoric cave signified past times, and past stages of consciousness.

It was obvious to him that his dream pointed to the foundations of cultural history, a history of successive layers of consciousness. Jung's dream thus constituted a kind of a structural diagram of the human psyche. It was his first inkling of a collective beneath the personal.

The discovery of the collective unconscious was critical. It represents a deep and timeless fund of human instincts and images in the psyche, which as you already know, Jung calls "archetypes". We probably wouldn't have this exclusive knowledge, or we would have it but within a more primitive framework, if Jung didn't interpret his fateful dream using nothing but the tool of his highly sensitive intuition. He could have just disregarded his night imagery as random nonsense. Sadly, a lot of people make this mistake.

However, he knew very well that the unconscious communicates through symbols and images, rather than coherent and consistent flow of data; regardless, one could achieve vast amounts of knowledge and wisdom by looking into this abstract pool of information.

Jung acknowledged that there was an underlying part of us which was interested in nothing else but the truth. The unconscious is ALWAYS interested in the Truth.

How did he know that? Well, he was one of the first people to check the physical indicators of a person while they were answering questions — sweat, pulse, temperature, etc. That means that he was one of the pioneers in the concept of a polygraph, or the so-called "lie detector".

Jung noticed that some answers made people more anxious, even though they were claiming to tell the truth —

something was happening on the inside, an inner conflict. And this underlying part of the psyche was revealing the resurging truth from the Deep, through physical indications and body language.

The Deep is always interested in revealing the truth about good and evil and everything in between. And this is why we should try and explore this realm, as difficult and incomprehensive as it may seem to be. It speaks the language of signs, symbols, images, sensations and feelings, and this is why it is so difficult to read. However, it is also connected directly with the Source. God sheds light to the channels of knowledge of those who search with pure hearts and ask Him for answers. Gradually, we learn to read and communicate in this symbolic and almost psychic language, just like we master any other language.

Our dreams often feel like scrambled gibberish, and there is a reason for that. Since the unconscious really is unconscious, and is very hard to access and decode, it discharges key symbols for you to find on the surface, in the form of a dream. And this is how the Deep speaks to you, giving you pieces of encoded knowledge about yourself. A knowledge that you don't know, don't realise or don't want to admit with your ego, in your awake state.

We forget the majority of our dreams; so the parts that come to the surface are those remainders that the Deep just cannot process, so it leaves it for our periphery conscious part to make sense of it, and to deal with it. In the same pattern, if you remember your dream and it lingers with you for months and even years afterwards, it must be important.

"A dream that is not understood remains a mere occurrence; understood it becomes a living experience." —

C.G. Jung

However, you can't always find the meaning immediately; sometimes the meaning of a symbol could be interpreted in time, when it suddenly feels more relevant and sensible. Very often the meaning is multi-layered, and a dream can also have more than one basic meaning. The meaning can change in time and take new nuances, as life progresses and becomes more saturated with new experiences. This is especially true for recurring dreams, or series of dreams, in which Jung was particularly interested.

Sometimes it is very hard to identify the meaning, but the reason for that is clear. People interpret the dream imagery literally or prophetically, without looking at the more abstract perspective. It has been proven that REM-sleep dreaming is associated with creative processes and abstract reasoning; this is why interpreting it in a very rigid and literal way wouldn't work most of the time.

You have to think out of the box and adopt a highly useful but also deeply gratifying appreciation for the metaphorical and symbolic way of expression. If you have that already, in your transcendence state your abstract thinking will take a new form — it will become especially powerful and will no longer feel and sound airy or unsubstantial to you, and to the people you speak with. Your abstract thought and the way you express it will become as concrete and logically coherent as an engineer explaining his plan with the use of a visible chart.

So how do you interpret dreams using abstract thinking? This process is closely related to the introspection that you are already familiar with. You go within. You peek into the Deep with the eyes of an innocent child. It is very important that first and foremost, you acknowledge that you (your ego) have no idea what that dream meant. You have to repeat it to yourself: "I have no idea what that dream meant." Only in this way can you block the path of your conscious ego which will immediately try to fill the gaps in a rational way and explain all symbols with the rational mind. The associations must really come from the deeply rooted intuition again.

"The dream is a little hidden door in the innermost and most secret recesses of the soul, opening into that cosmic night which was psyche (soul) long before there was any ego-consciousness, and which will remain psyche no matter how far our ego-consciousness extends." — C.G. Jung

You must direct your questions to the deepest parts of your psyche and accept the natural associations that inevitably swim up to the surface; sometimes they come as a feeling or as another more familiar symbol. We always start with the most personal interpretation. Surely, there are some basic and archetypal symbols that mean the same (or a very similar thing) to all of us, but this means that they would give you an exceedingly generic interpretation.

When you look at everything, even the archetypical, from a personal perspective — you will be as close to your own true personal interpretation as possible. For you the symbol of a dog might represent loyalty, friendship, companionship, but for another person scared of dogs with a childhood trauma, the appearance of a dog in a dream means enemy, threat, danger.

Most ancient cultures were fascinated with dreams; ancient Egyptians, for instance, wrote scripts with the interpretation of over a hundred dreams. But this was very limited as each dream was described to have only one single meaning, applicable to every human. This mistake has been repeated over and over again later on in history; even to this day there are some "fortune-telling" dream interpretation websites with universal explanations of dream symbols. In that sense Jung's insight that our night visions are highly personal was truly revolutionary.

"Dreams are impartial, spontaneous products of the unconscious psyche, outside the control of the will. They are pure nature; they show us the unvarnished, natural truth, and are therefore fitted, as nothing else is, to give us back an attitude that accords with our basic human nature when our consciousness has strayed too far from its foundations and run into an impasse." — C.G. Jung

I will provide you with some examples of basic archetypal symbols and what they represent in the generic abstract realm. I want you to think about what they represent to you specifically, and how you have experienced them in your own dreams.

I.   The four elements:

-       Earth — substantial, secure, brings you back to the ground, reality, materialism, growth, here and now, nurture, mother nature, mother, belonging, dirt, physical home, structured, eco-system, rigid, limited, lethargic.

-       Air — ideas, flying, possibilities, potentials, talents, experiments, view from the top, out of the box, limitless, energetic, fast, exciting, unsubstantial, not secure, no home to go to, scattered, unplanned, can fall down from too high.

-       Fire — passion, vehemence, ardour, fervour, desire, zest, zeal, burns, can grow into hate, dangerous, use with precaution, gives warmth, but dangerous when big, spreads fast, too strong to handle, only ashes remain in the end.

- Water — emotional state, world of feelings, sentiments, memories, could be calm but also stormy, could be clear but also muddy, could be a huge water pool or a small puddle, could be deep or shallow, gives life but also drowns people, strong but gentle, calming or dangerous, boundless, infinite, intelligent, secretive, serene.

II.	House/Castle/Villa — the psyche, the soul, the Inner Self. The different rooms or chambers represent different parts of the psyche; sometimes you may dream that you have new rooms in your house which just appeared, signalling an expanding consciousness or an acquired knowledge. The different floors represent the different layers of consciousness, just like in Jung's dream. The balcony is your connection with the outer world and with the Source — you are more exposed and vulnerable there, but also more receptive to the light and with a better vision of the horizon; yard — huge, small, non-existent? — could be the outer layer of your comfort zone and the connection between your safe space and others (also, is there any fence/ full visibility to the yard?); a thriving garden could be the thing in your psyche you tend to the most, or a dead garden could be a disregarded talent or potential.

III. Key — answer, secret, solution, clue, hint, cue, lead, the means of transitioning from one state to another, curiosity, movement, willingness to change, to seek, to explore, to learn, to unlock your potential, to open new doors and close old ones; but could also be the means of locking yourself inside four walls, putting up barriers, hiding secrets, hiding the Shadow self, lacking interest in going out of your comfort zone.

IV.	Tree — family, growth, life, connections, branches, network, people, cultures, nations, native lands, languages, knowledge, ancient, old, wise, solid, standing tall and strong, deep roots.

V.	Crash/Accident/Death — lack of control, losing

the game, losing the people you love, losing yourself, moving too fast, too reckless with something, unknown danger, unpredictability, fear of the unknown, fear of change, fear of the dark; but also, a cue that it's time for a certain part of you to be sacrificed and die.

VI.   Animals — depend on what they are and what they represent to you in your imagination, memories of previous experiences, personal feelings, affinities, fears, disgust.

VII.   Weapon — depends on who is holding it and what they intend to do with it; could be to kill — enemy, threat, animosity, aggression, hate, anger, primal instincts — or to scare something or someone off — protection, defence, vulnerability, fear, insecurity, being a target, a victim, defending your life/identity.

VIII.   Demon/Shadow/Ghost/Apparition — could be a product of your fear, or your own Shadow actually getting in touch with you through a dream. Do more and more shadow work if that keeps happening.

IX. Trip/Journey/Travelling   —   transitional state, movement, could be pleasant or scary if unknown; new challenges, new beginnings, escape, change for the better or for the worse, going out of your comfort zone for the better or for the worse, new contacts, new friends, new enemies, help on the way, problems on the way, forgetting the past, moving forward to the future.

These and many more symbols are very archetypical and common for all kinds of dreams and visions. It would be important to mention here that they do not only appear on the surface of your consciousness when you sleep. They also appear during creative processes and within your conscious search engine for ideas. For what it's worth, Jung also looked carefully into the schizophrenic visions and fantasies of his patients, as they held an equally important meaning for him. He saw these visions as bizarre emergences from the unconscious. He made his patients paint these images, turning them into real and externalised expressions and helping the patients to finally make sense of them, and relieve their symptoms a bit.

Being creatively triggered by the tendency to think in abstract terms, the archetypal symbols could be seen all too often in creative works of art — a painting of a stormy foamy ocean portrays the feelings of an angry painter; or a poem describing the burning fiery sensation of young lovers' desire for each other gives a sense of the poet's own inner fire.

Artists tend to "pull out" the exact symbol they need from the Deep and apply it to their masterpieces. Some particular artists like Leonardo had a gigantic talent in doing that, almost to the point where they seemed psychic.

Important archetypal symbols could be seen in my old writing as well which I described at the beginning of this book. The image of the hidden big castle represents the dark unconscious which we need to access and explore (the two boys finding each other); we also have to deal with our Shadow self along the way, and to overcome all dangerous challenges so that we can come back out as new people of the light. And I was just nine years old then. I am not even sure if I had understood completely how I came up with this relationship between the human psyche, all its processes, and these exact symbols.

The truth is there is no age limit in which we start receiving those basic meanings from the collective unconscious. This points out that we are able to begin our creative processes from a very young age. The full access to this world of ideas, possibilities, images and symbols predates the moment in which we actually become conscious, and this holds a huge meaning on its own. It proves the ancient nature of the collective unconscious (just like in Jung's dream), which directly connects to our creative minds. In this regard, I shall devote a separate chapter for creativity, as it is one of the most essential parts of human existence which proves the God particle in every one of us.

With dreams, it's not only about symbols — it's about the feelings they emanate. Have you ever dreamed of something mundane but throughout the whole dream you had this lurking feeling of threat or danger? Nothing really happened in the dream, but you woke up with this heavy feeling which lingered throughout your day. Same thing with happiness, or sadness, or excitement, or anxiety, or fear. Nightmares always affect the mood in a particularly bad way. You can also wake up with the sense of knowledge and discovery, and if you don't forget immediately what that is, you might be one of the few lucky ones. My favourite lingering feelings after a dream are the ones of relief and closure.

I will share with you one such dream of mine. It holds a strong personal meaning to me, and I was able to immediately interpret it without a struggle, right after it occurred. As you are reading it through, try it to do it yourself. It shouldn't be a huge struggle for you, given that you already know me too well.

I was nineteen or twenty and had just entered university, when I dreamed that I was my sixteen-year-old self again. I didn't see myself in the mirror, I just knew it and felt it.

I was out in my small home town which was gloomy and

unfriendly. I was heading towards the outskirts of the city and its exit. And then I started running — so quickly and effortlessly that it was actually enjoyable. My breath didn't get heavy, and a pleasant wind was blowing through my short hair as I was racing away from town. I felt excitement for what was upcoming.

Suddenly, I found myself in a new city I'd never been to, as I felt as if I had travelled a huge distance even though my sprint was just a few minutes long. The new city I was in felt very unfamiliar but very welcoming; it looked like a sunny Mediterranean place with no probability of bad weather, ever. The sun was gentle on my skin and I felt as if there was a big water body somewhere near, but I couldn't see it. And then I headed for an apartment somewhere near, because for some reason I knew that someone was waiting for me there.

I reached the block of flats, and it was in a bad condition — the building was tall and grey, old, with stains, and with broken parts unfixed in time. It was in contrast with the orange happy sense of the place outside and the weather. The front door of the building was slightly open, as if waiting for me to get in. I entered and the coolness of air shocked me a bit, but then I got used to it. I didn't use the elevator. I started climbing and climbing, aiming for the top floor. This time my breath got heavier with every step. I would stop for a rest from time to time, as the steps felt endless, but I knew I would somehow reach my goal at the end.

Upon reaching the top floor, I had become my twenty-year-old self again. When I reached the door of the apartment I was looking for, I saw none other but my sixteen-year-old self, waiting for me at the threshold...

I didn't know how that was possible, but it didn't feel

weird either. I knew that this was not an imposter: she had that same short dark haircut, and pale, hollow-cheeked face. She was slightly shorter, a bit too thin and stooped, and with too much dark eye makeup accompanied by a shiny metal piercing on her left eyebrow. She had that sad but also seeking look in her eyes — a glimmer of hope.

She wasn't smiling, she rarely did anyway; and she said nothing. I didn't ask her anything either; I already knew what I had to do.

She handed me a key, and I took it. Then she disappeared into thin air, when I unlocked the door and entered the apartment.

Not to my surprise, it was very unkempt and dark, dirty, messy and disorganised. Some parts of the furniture were missing, other parts were torn apart, there was no electricity, and the walls and floor were stained and mouldy. "OK, there is a lot of work to do, let's just get down to business," I thought.

But then my attention was seized by the shiny rays of light flowing into the living room through the balcony. The balcony looked so bright and welcoming that I couldn't resist checking it out before cleaning and organising the place. And so, I went out and I felt that warm and pleasant breeze again. More astonishingly, however, a huge body of water had just revealed in front of my eyes. I had felt it before, but now that I was so high above the ground, I could see it too. I was mesmerised by it. It was the most serene and calming blue that I had ever seen. It must have been an ocean, an infinite ocean. But it was so blue, so calm that it almost looked static; only the sun reflected beautifully on its surface, making the scene appear magical, wondrous, breath-taking. I stood there speechless and in pure bliss, taking in the light of the sun freely, and gazing into the beautiful horizon and beyond. My moments on this balcony felt uncountable, as if time had stopped — could have been seconds, minutes or hours.

When I entered the apartment back again, to my huge surprise — it was all cleaned up! It was cosy and welcoming, bright, new and clean — all of the furniture pieces were whole and in their right place. The walls were freshly painted. And there were plenty of new objects and cosy corners with bookshelves that hadn't been visible before.

It was as if everything had just magically fixed itself while I was in the light.

After this symbolic dream, I experienced a huge lingering relief, a feeling of strong confirmation of what I already knew, and a sense of closure mixed with enthusiasm for the future. I will always remember and cherish it.

Unfortunately, we won't be able to cover everything there is about symbols and dreaming, because it is a huge topic bordering on the spiritual but also fully enwrapped in the (meta)physical, medical and psychological. I can just advise you here to continue your reading on: dream states and stages, other archetypal symbols in dreams, Jung's guidebook for dream interpretation, prophetic dreams, nightmares and sleep disorders, sleep paralysis.

INSPIRATION AND CREATIVITY

"And He has filled him with the Spirit of God, with skill, with intelligence, with knowledge, and with all craftsmanship, to devise artistic designs, to work in gold and silver and bronze."
— Exodus 35:31-32

I knew that dreams were special long before I learned that Jung even existed. As a small child, I had many vivid and symbolic abstract dreams, and I would always look for the meanings. Fortunately, they were not accessible immediately. Even though I didn't have the answers, those colourful and bright night visions inspired me; and gave me some kind of abstract knowledge that I could only grasp slightly within the periphery of my child mind. And so I painted those visions — I used a lot of warm colours such as orange, red and pink, as they were always my favourite ones and this is how I saw the visions in my dreams.

My parents wondered at my imagination and didn't know why I was painting abstract forms and shapes in specific patterns, at the age of four. I didn't tell them either. My peers in the kindergarten would paint kittens or balloons or princesses, but I had no interest in that. I was exploring the connection between my inner database and my creativity, even back then. Moreover, I would also hear music in my dreams along with the shapes, and its frequencies matched perfectly the visual patterns. I just had to paint them; I felt the urge to externalise that.

I remember how we had an assignment in kindergarten to paint our favourite thing (a person, a pet, an activity, etc.) and I had painted my patterns again. The teacher looked at the other kids' paintings of mothers, kittens, houses and the like, and praised them for their creativity and effort.

When she came to see my painting, she frowned a bit and asked me what I was even painting. I answered enthusiastically: "Well, music, of course!" She didn't get it, frowned even more, and said nothing. She moved onto the next common painting. I took it very sensitively and felt awkward and disappointed. I felt as if I had deserved the praise but since she didn't understand my art and visions, maybe there was something wrong with me.

Many years later, I actually discovered that there was indeed something very different about me in that respect — I have the condition known as synaesthesia: a rather rare "blending" of the senses (originates from Greek with *syn* meaning "union", and *aesthesis* meaning "sensation": a union of the senses).

It explains why I have always "seen" patterns and colours within my mind's eye (inside my head) when I listen to music, even when I am not dreaming. And this is why all the graphemes (numbers and letters) have specific set colours for me, as well as personalities. It all made sense upon discovering synaesthesia later on in life, and everything sort of "clicked" for me.

Many synaesthetes grow up believing that everyone shares their complex associations and visions, and I was one of those believers. The inner connections just feel as natural and clear as reading a book. For better or for worse, this is not the case — not many people have synaesthesia. I was most probably the only child in my childhood circle who had this vivid inner world of connections and associations, and I had nobody to share it with. I don't think anybody would have understood it completely if I tried to, either.

Synaesthesia is fascinating. It is one of my main passions in psychology and life in general; it is very special to me on a personal level, as you can imagine. I have researched it so much that I would rather write a whole new book about it. It was the subject of my research in the Norwegian university I was invited to. I have investigated it through the psychological, neurological, artistic and spiritual perspectives. I believe it is very special, and it is yet another blessing from the Source which was given to me from the very beginning.

Not surprisingly, the Bible is written in synaesthetic terms as well:

- Ephesians 1:18: "I pray that the eyes of your heart may be enlightened..."

- Jeremiah 2:31: "O generation, see the word of the Lord..."

- Ecclesiastes 11:7: "How sweet is the light..."

There is one particular verse, Exodus 20:18 where the people went to Mount Sinai, and they experienced overwhelming synaesthetic sensations related to visual experiences caused by auditory stimuli, when God appeared to them:

"All the people saw the sounds and the lightning, the voice of the horn and the mountain smoking; and when the people saw it, they fell back and stood at a distance."

Synaesthesia is a mystery to this day. For me, synaesthesia represents a peculiar spiritual map; a delicate niche; a mental trajectory of the shortcut to God's presence. And that's why some people take hallucinogenic and recreational drugs in order to forcefully reach that state. They want to engage in this intertwining of colours, shapes, words, and sounds, and they don't assess the consequences of this ego assertion into a world they know nothing about.

Synaesthesia also has practical use. The condition provides me with a "cheat" to the game, to be honest. It does give me an easier, clearer and more direct access than most people, to the creative chaotic world of the unconscious from where I pull my ideas. It also represents a free tool for decoding the symbols emerging from the Deep, no matter how complex they might be. I already have the neurological connections and associations useful for the act of creation, for which other people must work extra to achieve. Synaesthesia feels like an instant metaphorical expression in your mind without putting an effort to make up the metaphor.

A lot of famous artists, scientists, writers, poets, musicians and composers were confirmed or speculated to have this unique condition. Amongst the confirmed cases are: Van Gogh, Vladimir Nabokov, Nikola Tesla, Franz Liszt, Duke Ellington, Richard Feynman, Wassily Kandinsky, Olivier Messiaen, and many others. Leonardo is speculated to have had it as well.

However, I do not believe that you have to be a synaesthete in order to achieve greatness in the act of creation. Training your brain in synaesthesia surely helps and has proven to increase your IQ slightly. However, we all have the necessary basic tools apart from it, which help us read the symbolic language of the Deep and apply it to our art.

These tools are called talents and we all have the responsibility to develop them and use them accordingly. They were gifts from the Source, and a universal method for us to see through our unique mission. Your talents are always the most accurate indicator of what your mission is mapped out to be, on this plane of existence.

Talents don't always have to be related to art, and that is why I use the term act of creation, as talents are always related to the act of creation.

"Art isn't only a painting. Art is anything that's creative, passionate, and personal. And great art resonates with the viewer, not only with the creator... An artist is someone who uses bravery, insight, creativity, and boldness to challenge the status quo. And an artist takes it personally." — Seth Godin

These unique inner tools called talents are amongst the strongest proof that God lives in all of us — as he was the original Creator; the original Life Source. Some people wrongly assume that they don't have any talents, but usually those people are the ones who don't know themselves at all. They have done zero self-reflection and exploration and have chosen the lazy and shallow way of living. Talents have no limits and restrictions, and could be found in all eight types of intelligence:

- Logical-mathematical intelligence
- Linguistic intelligence
- Spatial intelligence
- Musical intelligence
- Bodily-kinesthetic intelligence
- Interpersonal intelligence (with other people)
- Intrapersonal intelligence (within yourself)
- Naturalistic intelligence

Which types of intelligence do you find applicable to

your own mind, soul and personality? What talents do you express within each of your strong intelligences? Do you have hidden talents, or such that have been repressed over the years?

If yes, you should find a way to express them, as they are the tools for accomplishing your mission. If you have not utilised your talents, it means that you are not crafting the right product according to the right chart, using the right tools.

Besides, there is no greater gratification than the feeling after you have exhausted your creative energy flowing from this talent. It feels as if you have finally done the right thing, and you can rest for a bit until your reservoir is filled up again. And as you may have discovered, this reservoir fills up very quickly, ready to support the act of creation again and again.

Creativity and talents can also be applied in the way you lead your business; in the way you creatively come up with a breakthrough idea for your next project that will lead you to big profits.

The act of creation is very visible in brainstorming sessions of all kinds, and the concept of the "hive mind" is also present in such scenarios. It has been proven that the group IQ in a brainstorming session is much higher than the IQs of its individual participants. Creativity and imagination play the biggest role in solving problems and coming up with solutions — whether it is in mathematics, or life. Maths and life are intertwined anyway, so think about it next time your child complains how they would never apply that "useless" equation in real life.

Creativity could be found in dance — the movement of the body, the unique trajectories it makes and the patterns it creates with its dynamic movements. More often than not, dancers are unaware of these patterns; as everything flows from the unconscious and is hard to spot by many people, including the performers themselves.

Creativity is evident in sports, especially in those requiring strategy and planning in combat, endurance, or teamwork. People possessing the bodily-kinesthetic intelligence, which is crucial for sports, express their talents in a unique way; but are often underappreciated in their artistic performance. The reason is that sports are the most externalised and materialistic way in which you can express the ideas you have pulled from the distant unconscious, applying them in your performance. The connection is a huge stretch; the line is very thin and barely visible but it's definitely existent. Especially if we are talking about the link between team sports and hive-mind theory.

Another reason is that many sports are very dynamic and fast, and they don't remain in time in order to be appreciated, and re-appreciated, as a work of art. But that doesn't mean that they are not an act of creation; it is not by chance that martial arts are called exactly like this. It's the same creative and unconscious, imaginative process. Instinct itself, and even peripheral reflexes, are in direct interaction with your unconscious self which acts for you sometimes; not to forget that the unconscious is interested in the truth, and in self-protection.

It is almost as if you have two personas in you: one above, and one below the surface — and the one below is the one with the age-old ideas and symbols, but also with the active present instincts, much faster than the stream of thought of your conscious ego-mind. The Deep is where you are at this present moment, but also where you have always been ever since you were born and before, and where you will always be in this lifetime and after you die.

Creativity is definitely seen in humour and jokes too! In fact, it is very healthy to make up jokes about different scenarios, as the required way of thinking is insightful and inventive, as you make unique connections that weren't there before. Sense of humour is really important and surely related to the artistic way of thinking, operating partly in the unconscious realm. What the best comedians do is truly art, and you can feel it in the way they structure and present the joke. Their best jokes are always wrapped in symbols, metaphors and imagery, as you almost feel the story unfolding in front of you as if on film.

Imagination and inspiration could be, and should be, applied to science as well. This is actually what separates real science from fake. Tesla was a real scientist; he was able to see what's behind the veil thanks to his additional senses, and the way he naturally pulled ideas from the Deep on a massive scale. He obviously knew, or rather saw, something that the majority of other scientists didn't. He was almost psychic in the way he saw the world, experienced numbers, explained energies.

Tesla was apparently greatly inspired by something in order to go into this unusual path of science, and that is why his life and work have been shrouded in so much mystery to this day. He saw patterns invisible to other people, he pulled ideas out of seemingly nowhere, and he was inside his head most of the time. This creative and inspired energy flowed through him, stronger and brighter than the electric charges he so thirstily researched, and made it impossible for him not to act on his talents while fulfilling his mission.

"There is a vitality, a life force, an energy, a quickening

that is translated through you into action, and because there is only one of you in all time, this expression is unique. And if you block it, it will never exist through any other medium and will be lost." — Martha Graham

Inspiration can come in many ways, shapes and forms. It's the muse that people of art have talked about since the dawn of time. It's that "random" single sound which is just the right pitch for the musician to come up with a whole beautiful composition. It's that specific shade of blue that gives the artist a stream of invisible symbolic information and brings him to paint an abstract masterpiece. It's those bright words and chants of phrases that linger inside a poet's mind and become heavier and heavier, until they are put on paper.

Inspiration is of a Latin origin/inspirare/ and originally means "Divine guidance". For me, the concept of inspiration has always stood within a closely associated and joint network with the word enthusiasm — of a Greek origin/enthous/ which originally means "Possessed by God".

You can be struck by inspiration and feel a sudden enthusiasm without even knowing why, and in the most unexpected moment. But it is important to seize this moment and proceed with your act of creation — no matter what it is. If the circumstances do not allow immediate expression, make sure that you at least write your idea, map it out in your head or on paper, make a voice recording of what you are inspired and enthusiastic to do.

Cherish your inspirations, as they usually come from the Source. They are prompts of action, unlike any other; they are significant and sometimes fateful pushes that dictate your whole course of life, possibly the lives of others too. Just think about all those examples in history when the whole course of humanity changed after a single moment of inspiration…

Inspiration comes in dreams too. We already discussed how some people wake up with a knowledge that they didn't have before they went to sleep. They may have accidentally decoded the symbolic language of unconscious dreams, and now their conscious minds have the intelligible answers. But not for too long. If you've had such instances, you may already know how difficult it is to grasp this knowledge which came from the depths, for more than one minute. Make sure you write down everything the second you wake up, otherwise there is a risk of forgetting it immediately. The unconscious truths are like fish — they can't live for too long outside the vast ocean, unless you make the effort and put them in your very own bowl of water.

There is one particular stage of sleep in which this kind of magic happens: the hypnagogic state. Hypnagogia is the transitional state between wakefulness and sleep. All kinds of people report having strong visual (and sound) imagery during those initial moments of sleep; while the brain is still at alpha (relaxation) waves, but also suddenly at theta waves (characterised by the onset of REM sleep).

This could include the most common "hypnagogic jerk" — rapid muscle spasm after a dream sensation of a fall or a bump; loud non-existent noises, or images of bright lights or even explosions that wake you up ("the exploding head syndrome") or lead you to deeper sleep depending on the intensity of the experience. Colourful patterns during hypnagogia are also common. Images of archetypal symbols, personal signs and mind mappings are also very frequently experienced by hypnagogic sleepers.

Hypnopompia is the exact opposite transitional state of

awakening from sleep, in which similar imagery is reported to take place.

Part of my research in Norway was related to hypnagogia as well; in fact, I managed to discover a connection between synaesthesia and hypnagogia. The relationship between the two is fascinating. There are some people who actually do not experience synaesthesia in their awakened state; however, they experience it only as they drift off to sleep — in their hypnagogic transition; and they truly refer to their state as "hypnagogic synaesthesia". For example, they hear a real loud noise from the outside world which sometimes jerks them awake, other times not, but they always experience visual patterns caused by the real sound.

One of my participants in my qualitative research reported to see different shapes and forms appearing in consequence to the different external noises. He said that if he would hear a high-pitched sound, the visual pattern in his hypnagogic state would look like long and thin two-dimensional lines — either zig-zag or straight, depending on the change in the pitch. A lower and quieter sound would bring up rounder shapes in darker, softer shades. Another female participant reported that the sounds of a bird chirping next to her window while she was transitioning to sleep would cause her visions of colourful raindrops inside her mind.

I read an additional report online of a girl who devoted her thesis to the subject, researching everything that is out there about hypnagogia, because she experienced it a lot. Without the trigger of an outer sound or noise, she would actually hear "inner music" in her transition to sleep and see those strange but beautiful colourful patterns during her hypnagogic state. She would describe them as "geometrically perfect and very pleasant to observe".

Upon reading this, I immediately thought about my own dreams as a child, as it appears that there is a striking similarity between her experiences and mine. However, my dreams gradually faded over time and my awakened synaesthesia remained. With her, the dreams remained throughout childhood and adolescence, and into young adult years; but she didn't appear to have the standard sound-to-image synaesthesia (chromesthesia) in her awakened state.

There is another difference, as well — I do remember that I experienced those dreams in my deep sleep state, possibly REM, unlike her visions during her transitional hypnagogic state. Nonetheless, the visions are the same, and they came to us both from the collective unconscious myriad of ideas, mystical symbols and mathematical patterns.

I know that there is another more general connection between synaesthesia and hypnagogia; and I was able to prove it with the help of my cooperative and honest participants whom I recruited for my research. Both synaesthetes and hypnagogic sleepers (often the two coincide) have a stronger inner imagery than the average person.

What that means is that if you make them imagine a scenery of nature and describe it to you — they report invoking the image inside their head immediately and without any difficulty or effort; and are able to describe it down to the tiniest detail. Furthermore, they often describe the sensation of almost "being there" — immersed in the scenery, even though they are aware that they are just imagining it.

For me, strong imagery means better skills at withdrawing symbolic and visual language from the Deep and immersing yourself into the images. Strong imagery means inevitable creativity and a need for expression of that innately generated creative energy. Imagery is also related to imagination, however, imagination has the connotation of craftsmanship by utilising what you already have; while imagery is all about pulling out what is not yours yet — what is still hidden in the Deep, before you reach out to it.

Metaphors are a special kind of such imagery, wrapped up in the linguistic, sensational, artistic and spiritual. Metaphoric expressions are yet another product of almost magical imagery skills, of invoking just the right association at the right time. Since the connection is established once, it stays there, noticed and acknowledged by appreciative and receptive artistic souls later on in history. Both poets and prose writers thrive in the metaphorical. Shakespeare was a master at that:

"Out, out, brief candle! Life is but a walking shadow, a poor player that struts and frets his hour upon the stage and then is heard no more…" — Macbeth

Strong imagery is important for the synaesthetic and the hypnagogic state (or is it the other way around?). One reason for that is that hypnagogia, just like synaesthesia, is also a gift from the Source that could be used practically. A lot of deep visions come to the periphery of the mind during the hypnagogic state, and this is why so many people get their immediate answers while falling asleep and are able to remember them for a bit longer than usual.

The most common scenario is a person who drifts off to sleep while researching his subject of interest, trying to solve a problem, or to answer a question. And as he drifts off, the answer emerges from the Deep and swims all the way up to the surface — where the conscious mind picks it up and processes it. We always have the answers inside; the unconscious is always interested in the truth — it's just that our ego doesn't always allow the truth to come to the surface.

The "drifting off technique" became so commonly successful for scholars, thinkers, scientists and artists that they would intentionally induce those naps in the midst of solving a problem or coming up with an idea.

Hypnagogia was how Mary Shelley caught sight of the vision that led her to write *Frankenstein*. Robert Louis Stevenson, the writer of none other than the absolutely archetypical story of *The Strange Case of Dr Jekyll and Mr Hyde*, systematically relied on hypnagogic states to come up with complete concepts for his books. Beethoven and Dali also credited this phenomenon with assisting their creativity. Dmitri Mendeleev is said to have visualised how to arrange his Periodic Table of Elements while drifting off to sleep in his chair one afternoon.

There is a theory that hypnagogia and hypnapompia produce nothing else but the visual equivalents for one's own deepest emotions and thoughts — the ones that you can find far lower down the cave from Jung's dream.

There is a theory that synaesthesia is the sign of humans being in active real-time evolution, that is more spiritual than anything else. It is not by chance that all synaesthetes I found for my research were very interested in the artistic and the spiritual, in one way or another. Many of them stated that it is an inseparable part of them.

These phenomena, these unique mysteries related to imagery, creativity, inspirations, visions and art — pose more questions than we have answers to. The conditions are not researched thoroughly enough, and to this day are shrouded in mystery in their most important component — the spiritual one.

However, I feel that they represent a stronger expression of what all of us have — an ability to peek inside the Deep and get our answers from there in the form of symbols and images. We all can do that through dreams, through active conscious seeking, through metaphorical and abstract associations, and as a result of divine inspirations which come just in time. Our responsibility is to always understand what we already have, and what we are willing to explore even further. Only in this way we can put everything to good use and in accordance with our talents, in our unique act of creation. And we must always act within the limits of our potential.

In the next chapter, I will acquaint you with a different kind of people: people with a wider, unlocked potential. Those people are real, and all of them existed on Bulgarian lands. Their stories are still told across the country. People from the older generations who knew them directly or indirectly still share the tales of those mystics' developed inner senses.

Those people had stronger energies and functioned on higher frequencies. More importantly, they had direct access to the unconscious, not only when they were asleep, or in a hypnagogic or inspired state. The images they pulled from the Deep were sometimes unintelligible and overwhelming even to them. However, they could see through the dark hazy pool of the unconscious as clearly as if they were looking through a glass. Those people were definitely gifted ones, and they had very special missions...

PHENOMENA

"The most beautiful experience we can have is the mysterious. It is the fundamental emotion that stands at the cradle of true art and true science." — Albert Einstein

Baba Vanga

Vangelia Gushterova, later known as Baba Vanga, was born in 1911 in a small village in southern Bulgaria, near the Rupite Mountains. She was a premature baby and unlikely to live, but she survived. In Bulgaria, at that time, there was a tradition not to name the baby before there was certainty that he or she would live. She was named Vangelia, from "Evangelos" (Greek), meaning "the messenger of good news".

Vangelia had a difficult childhood within a poor family, as did most Bulgarian children at that time. Life has never been easy on our lands. Her father was in the army participating in World War One, sometimes gone for months. Her mother died when she was a small child. Vanga had to take care of herself from a very young age, without much external help. Still, she managed to live a happy life, she lived close to nature and appreciated the small things. She had friends, neighbours and distant relatives, so it wasn't as if she was completely alone.

Vanga was considered intelligent and insightful for her age. Her inclinations started to show up when she invented games and played "healing" — she prescribed some herbs to her friends, who pretended to be ill. It was very obvious that she had a developed naturalistic type of intelligence and healing talents from a small age. This is not uncommon at all on Bulgarian lands, as there is a myriad of healing herbs only found on our side of the Balkans. They are almost magical, almost alive, with their breath of aroma and healing effects. And because of this, it is very logical that there will be more souls incorporated with naturalistic knowledge about herbs and natural medicine — knowledge which, of course, also comes intuitively.

We have always had people who can "see" the connection between specific herbs and specific illnesses; or even if there is no illness, they still know what kind of tea to prescribe to you so that you can make your organ stronger and healthier. This is a very high level of naturalistic intuition which is hard to explain in simple terms. Only when official research is made can you see scientifically how the herb is confirmed to help with the specific problem. But this is the thing: more often than not, it's the simplest villagers living close to nature in Bulgaria who have this inner natural knowledge; and I doubt that they have ever seen a single official scientific proof about it. This special treasure of hidden knowledge is also passed down from generation to generation, and it will never die in Bulgaria. Personally, I have spoken to at least five people of different ages who have deep knowledge about herbs and natural healing; and all of them are right on point. But I digress.

Vanga was growing up and nothing too special was taking place. And then in her teenage years, the unthinkable happened…

Vanga was in the fields and she sensed that a storm was imminent. She tried to hurry home, but the wind was suddenly so strong that she had a hard time even walking. Dust, soil and sticks were bumping into her face and it was difficult for her to see. Everything was happening too quickly. It was almost as if the force of nature was gaining control over her at an instant. The powerful wind started twisting around her and lifted her off her feet. She was losing all control and was in the hands of destiny. The tornado twisted her ceaselessly and took her higher and higher, until she lost consciousness.

Vanga had no way of knowing about the tornado — as it formed around her, in real time. We never have tornados in Bulgaria. This happens rarer than once in a blue moon. What happened to Vanga was bizarre and unexplained to this day.

She was found after several days unconscious, weary and injured, thrown away from the twister on the next field. Vanga had lost her sight almost entirely. All the dust and particles had attacked her vision and injured her eyes badly. She gradually lost her eyesight completely in the upcoming months.

What Vanga gained with her vision loss was another type of vision. She suddenly began "seeing" things that were beyond the three-dimensional reality which we absorb with our five senses, predominantly with our eyesight. She sensed patterns, energies, signs and prospects for the future. Vanga predicted the future easily and always presented it in symbols — because this is the language of the unconscious. Her predictions for the future are studied to this day, and the majority of them have already occurred just as she predicted or are going to occur in the near future.

After the fateful incident, her whole life took a turn. She didn't have any personal life now — she lived for others. Rumours were spreading fast, and only from word to mouth suddenly everyone knew about Vanga and her powers. People from all over Bulgaria would come to visit her, forming a queue in front of her house, every single day for years to come. A lot of people wanted to hear about their future, they had problems and were desperate to reach out to Vanga for help, guidance and healing. My own grandmother managed to meet Vanga when Vanga was in her late years, in the beginning of the 1990s. My grandmother used to have some powers as well, not nearly as activated as Vanga's, but Vanga helped her with answers about that.

Vanga became so prominent that renowned politicians from the Soviet Union and the West came to visit her. They would come for advice and were dying to hear out her symbolic predictions. Vanga made many accurate predictions over the years about the political, military and economic state of Bulgaria, Russia, Europe and the whole world. She would warn world leaders not to do a certain political or military move before this move was even announced as a potentiality.

Vanga also had healing powers and she could allegedly see when a person was going to die — almost like a lifeline in her inner vision. That is why she refused to receive people who were already too sick when they came for a visit and were going to pass away in the following days or weeks. And indeed, they did — but she never told them, as it was forbidden, she believed. Vanga could sense the person's presence from the outside and often knew who was going to enter her room and for what, even though she had never met them. She already knew their whole story, so she would immediately come up with the answer, or with the right healing.

Vanga's wisdom and "seeing" powers were inspiring but also frightening, because she just knew too much. That is why she was invited to participate in the projects of the scientific community at the most prominent Bulgarian institute at that time, but she refused.

Everyone was aware that Vanga was keeping a lot to herself. She didn't tell the whole story of her visions and symbols and made it obvious that not everything is sharable.

Even though Vanga felt overloaded with these additional senses, she never cursed her own fate. She knew that part of her mission was to overcome the difficulties designed only for her life. She also felt alone. When one knows more than the others, he or she can't help but feel alone. Vanga's mission was not easy and she walked in pain rather than happiness. However, even though she was physically blind, she had her inner eyes opened, and she knew what it was all about.

Vanga was a strong believer in Christ — after all, how can she not be? She always prayed and asked for permission and forgiveness; she was aware that her gift was given to her at a price, and she was careful. Most importantly, Vanga endured it all and managed to stay wise, calm and gathered until her very end, in 1996. She was an extremely strong woman — the real kind of strong, which is very easily distinguishable from the modern distortion of "strong, independent" women who are actually unstable, triggered and offended by every little thing.

The story about the blind mystic Baba Vanga sounds like a fairy tale but it is absolutely real — she is a phenomenon unlike any other on planet earth. A lot of old and recent documentaries have been made about Vangelia Gushterova, and I believe a lot more should be done in the future, as there is a lot more to investigate. What is certain is that after the incident Vanga received an unimaginably easy, and possibly full, access to her symbolic and figurative unconscious. In addition, her direct channel with the Source was extremely clear, unlike our partly blurry but otherwise reliable intuition. Vanga had these additional senses which she utilised as naturally as we utilise our eyesight. Above all, Vanga was humble and righteous, and never used her powers for her own gain.

Vanga was here to help others in an unprecedented way: she was the messenger of good news, but also of harsh warnings if we do not change on time. Vanga was here to change people's way of thinking, so that they can change their own destinies and walk on the right path again. She was here to give out her life to the people, at the expense of her own happiness. A modern-day martyr, who was the chosen one by fate to influence thousands of people — not only because of what happened to her, but especially because of her intrinsic righteousness, naturalistic talents and saint-like wisdom.

Slava Sevryukova

Slava was born in 1905, in the small Bulgarian town of Nova Zagora, close to the Balkan mountain chain. The etymology of her name comes from Eastern Orthodox, and literally means "honour, fame, glory".

Slava was born into a poor but gifted family. Both her grandmother and mother had the gift, but with Slava it was multiplied by dozens. Her grandmother was a master at alternative medicine and herbology. Her mother could predict the future and people's fates. Slava could do all of those things and more, from a very young age. Rumours were spreading fast about her powers, and her family didn't want her to be deemed as sorceress. So they quickly decided to make a life for her and marry her to a man prematurely.

Slava was just 16 when she married the Ukrainian emigrant Stepan Sevryukov — he was twenty years older than her. Their problems started soon after. He was a jealous, short-tempered, and obsessive man, with a weakness for alcohol. Slava did not trust him and tried to hide her special powers from him. However, people naturally gathered around her, because they felt her light, and she would openly accept them at home. There was no way in which her husband wouldn't notice her clairvoyant tendencies, as oblivious as he may have been. He got more and more angry and jealous, and forced her to move places on several occasions, as she kept attracting people without even trying.

They moved to Knyazhevo and Slava had to start work at a textile factory, which was a difficulty. Because of the chemicals she worked with there, she suffered from illnesses of her liver and she had seven subsequent operations. She also lost her ability to have children. The problems with her husband didn't stop even then, as he would continue to disrespect her, fight with her and drink even more heavily.

Her friends urged Slava to divorce him, but she wouldn't listen; she was aware that she was cleansing her soul by going through this marital difficulty. Slava was sure that her soul was the one who chose this specific earthly experience in order to make a difference in this lifetime. She felt that she shouldn't give up on her husband, and she was indeed by his side to the very end, until he died.

Slava's spirit was caring, calm and gathered; she was the epitome of patience and resilience. Slava was famous for being very humble and modest. She was extremely strong and could magically mobilise herself to keep going no matter what. With each destruction that came her way, she managed to construct everything again from scratch, with the power of love and faith. She always knew the bigger meaning behind her suffering, and this is how it was all bearable. Even though she had only graduated fourth grade, she was also highly intelligent and unimaginably insightful against all probabilities. Slava was a wise old soul with a gift of knowledge from out of this world but relating to this world precisely.

One of her greatest powers was to clearly "see" the microcosmos of our universe. She would describe in great detail how the atom was structured, even though she never reached the point of learning about it at school. Her mind's eye just had the special ability to "zoom into" the smallest particles of our matter, and clearly see all the patterns, geometrical structures and perfect symmetries. Slava knew how each element of the periodic table looked, felt and smelled like, without being exposed to it physically. She could "feel" the texture, "see" the colour and the structure, and "smell" the odour.

Everything pointed out to the fact that apart from her well-functioning five outer senses, she had all five inner senses developed as well, as a mirror projection. However, the second set of senses was even stronger, as it also allowed her to zoom into the matter, almost like a human microscope. These inner senses also seemed to blend as well; in fact, her abilities remind me of some special clairvoyant type of synaesthesia — she got all types of sensory stimuli just by being exposed to a single mental concept (e.g., the idea of a specific type of metal).

Not to forget, her gift also allowed her to foresee the probabilities for the future as if on frames. From her own description, it becomes clear that she may have had access to the original charts for what was upcoming. It is a common theo-philosophical theory that before the material events happen in the physical realm, they are first "recorded" in the spiritual; and only a handful of souls have access to that original source.

Slava was especially good at decoding symbolism, as this is how she received her messages, and this is how she saw the truths inside the pool of her unconscious. She probably had the most transparent access to the Deep, and she was also blessed with the ability to decode its profound figurative messages. This is why she had the ability to see through the Bible's symbolism and interpret it in a very unique way. Slava would decipher each sign and story and ascribe their precise meanings.

Her myriad of powers was getting stronger with the years, and she was gaining more and more popularity, similarly to Vanga. (The two clairvoyants actually knew each other, and what Vanga had said about Slava was that everything she uttered was the truth.) Prominent people would come to Slava for clairvoyance and predictions. Journalists would take long interviews with her; writers would get inspired and write whole books about her. Physicists, historians and engineers would make documentaries for her. Slava even got some academic recognition from both Bulgarian and international institutes and organisations — from Russia, Spain, India. The simple, small-town woman, who had only finished grade four…

Slava was a humble Christian and didn't take the fame too seriously. Her mere motivation was to give out her whole existence for the sake of people, and for the sake of the Divine Plan. She was aware that her mission was to redeem herself from mistakes in her past lifetimes and cleanse her soul for good. It is not by chance that she couldn't have children — her struggles but also powers ended with her, as this is how it was designed to be. After her lifetime, those powers were probably not necessary anymore.

In that sense, Slava knew that there was always a connection between everything; she could see those strings of connection in our reality. With her gentle and wise nature, she would help people psychologically too by reminding them of this simple truth. She would explain how all difficulties and problems happened for a reason; bad always comes from something unresolved and when it happens, it is actually good for the soul. It means that the soul gets cleansed from past mistakes.

Slava lost her powers for two years because she overstepped one important universal law. However, she learned from her mistake and prayed in humility. After the sudden loss of her powers, Slava reported feeling as if someone had "cut off her vital strings with scissors", and she felt miserable about it. She felt as if she was missing senses, even though physically she was a human being like every other. Slava got the vision that her powers would return when a man with a specific soft hat on his head would appear in her life. After that vision, she was curious to look for that person. She didn't do it actively, but she would be attentive while walking in a crowd, or when she met new people. However, Slava didn't see the person from her vision anywhere, as more than two years passed. She continued to pray and repent.

And then on one winter night, a woman she knew knocked on her door for an unannounced visit, bringing a man with her. She wanted Slava to meet the man and help him with something. As the man came into the house, she immediately recognised him: the man from her vision with the same soft hat. And from this moment on, Slava describes, her powers charged into her again — mightier than ever. Slava describes this transformation as "seeing" once again. Her powers never left her after that.

She had a very special connection with one honest and dedicated scientist and engineer — Ivo Lozenski. They met in 1962, when Ivo was a 28-year-old assistant at the Geological Institute in Sofia. He was interested in meeting Slava, as he was researching similar things, and he had heard about her visions. He was amazed by Slava's ability to scan the three-dimensional space, invisible to the human eye. Ivo also wondered at her ability to be freely transferred to the past, present, future; to sense and control frequencies.

What began was a life-long tandem, a partnership of a scientist and a clairvoyant. Everything she described in her simple terms, he confirmed in engineering and physical terms. Ivo applied the approaches of psychotronics, in order to explain the structure of our micro cosmos and the ethereal structure of our reality using nothing but her visions and his background knowledge. She would help him with his research, and he would publish everything they have concluded by working together. Their findings bordered the quantum realm, the spiritual, and also the strictly physical. Their research was innovative, break-through, and multi-layered. In my opinion, their work still hasn't got the popularity it deserves. Or it could be that humanity is still not ready for it.

He stayed with her until the very end of her life in 1991, as Slava had accepted him as her son. He would take care of her with her progressing old age, exactly as a son would. He was loyal, empathetic and kind — and this is why Slava had chosen him, she would say; even though dozens of renowned physicists, engineers and biologists had wanted to work closely with her, especially after she got her recognition. She had chosen him because of his honesty and good heart. Slava had attracted good people around her, but Ivo was the closest thing to a family.

Slava had an incredible, otherworldly intuition that I doubt could be even deemed as intuition. It was an overly acute set of additional five senses that she had on the inside. This was noticed and acknowledged by real scientists who knew that she had something to say, and something more to see. They could have judged the book by its cover and said that nothing new could come out of an uneducated woman's mouth. But it was difficult to sustain ego when close to such a bright and strong presence. Even the most rigid and closed-minded materialists felt that there was something about her. She managed to break through all the barriers and intertwine with real science and breakthrough research.

Slava was the honourable, gentle soul who learned from her past mistakes, and awakened a lot of people on her path. She was a generous and righteous person, who accepted people in distress at her home until the very end, even though she could hardly walk and talk. Slava was a fragile woman, and a strong fighter; she was an unyielding believer in Christ, and an empathetic intuitive leader. Stories are still circulating around the country by people who have met her personally, and who have interviewed her in the past.

Slava was here to investigate our world more deeply than everyone else before her; so deeply, in fact, that she literally used a "zoom in" instrument. Apart from her acute inner senses, she had the knowledge and the wisdom to remind people what our material reality truly represents, and what our own existence is all about. Slava was the humble fragile woman who had the difficult mission to get so many people back on their feet again, even though her own personal path was a hard one. She was a reminder of the truth that we always somehow forget about having a good heart and doing the right thing no matter what. And one does not need to know the structure of the atom to be aware of that.

Vera Kochovska

Vera Kochovska was born in 1945 in a small Bulgarian town near the capital Sofia. She had a very difficult childhood, as her father died when she was little, and her mother abandoned her right after. She was then put into foster care and had to learn how to be a fighter from a very young age. "Vera" is a dialectic word of "faith" in Bulgarian.

When she was 13 years old, Vera had an accident. She was hit by a truck on the road, and she almost died. She was in a coma for two whole months and had many broken bones. While Vera was in a coma, her spirit escaped from her body and she could see her physical body from above. Just as many people with near-death experiences report, Vera could also see and hear all the doctors and nurses that came in and out of her hospital room. During her clinical death, Vera also reports heading to a tunnel with a very bright light on the other side. She started walking through it and a powerful feeling of endless love and calmness overwhelmed her. Vera sensed other souls' presence, some of her deceased relatives and also people she didn't know; but all of them accepting, loving, calm, welcoming. She saw them all as energies, as beings of light, as they had no physical forms, but she knew who they were... or used to be. Even though the thought to stay there in the light was alluring, she knew that it was still not her time to pass on.

This brief contact with the netherworld changed Vera forever. As her spirit returned to her physical body, this otherworldly sense got back along with it. When she came to her senses, her eyes had suddenly turned blue from brown. Vera could somehow "see" people's organs. Doctors and nurses would come to help her, and she would tell them where they had health problems in their bodies, and what was going to happen in their lives. She wasn't scared; she had a deep subconscious understanding of the meaning of her sudden gift. Vera also reports receiving a mature wisdom uncharacteristic of her fragile 13 years of age. She had an immediate and full understanding of her mission after she came back from death.

Vera could diagnose but also heal. She started healing people immediately, even the most hopeless cases of sick patients. People would come to her so that she can fix the smallest problems, or just to receive hope from this wise young woman with a very old soul. Vera would gladly heal people; but was very vocal about the fact that physical sickness comes from a disturbance in the soul, and from uncleaned darkness. She could only do so much with the little time that was given her on planet Earth, but she had a vision for something more; she wanted to fix the core problem.

Vera wanted to open people's eyes to the truth about good deeds, pure love, forgiveness, faith, and gratuitous help. She strived to awaken people to the fact that the spiritual and the material realms are intertwined, and you can't escape from that; this is why evil when untreated translates into physical sickness, and unfortunately goes down the generation line. Vera felt hurt from all the animosity, aggression, hatred and anger; she was very sensitive but at the same time unyielding in her statements of how pernicious all that is. Vera loved the people but hated their sins; she was over-receptive of every little evil spot in the soul of a person and would directly tell them what it is and how to fix it, if their ego allowed it.

Vera would sometimes feel the whole of humanity's wrongdoings lying on her shoulders. She would feel the burden of that and would often say how what she had was not a gift but a huge load to carry. Vera was extraordinary in every way, and this is why people of all sorts (good and bad) would come to her for advice and healing. She always had this deep knowledge which never lifted the heaviness off her eyes. Vera regularly talked about our Creator and the missions he assigned us with; and it hurt her to see such a significant number of people "spit" on their missions and prefer the wrong frivolous lifestyle. She was, of course, able to see all persons' original designs and mission charts — and it was probably very painful to see how the ego distorted that original purity and beauty and turned it into a hateful and boastful life.

Just like Slava and Vanga, Vera also had a contribution in real science; not as big as it should have been, however. With what she offered to science, she should have been world-famous, but mainstream science and media doesn't want you to hear about key human phenomena like her. Same goes for the other phenomena of Bulgaria and the Balkans. Vera, Slava and Vanga may have been some of humanity's direct links to the other world, to Heaven, to the deep unconscious, to the truth, to everything invisible. And they never got popular enough to the point where they were studied as phenomena and described in books and chronicles enough as changers of human destinies.

Even though some experiments were indeed done on Vera, they were far away from sufficient, taking into account what she had to offer with her spiritual strength and otherworldly knowledge. More attention should be brought to people like her, who were the true influencers in history, even if it is on a small, national scale. And what we get now is hundreds of superficial and fake Instagram "influencers" who are anything but important to the history of humanity. Do you see how wrong the majority of modern media is? But I digress.

The experiments with Vera Kochovska in Bulgaria began in 1989 at the University of Shumen's laboratory. The results were so impressive that they changed the opinions of the biggest sceptics of Vera's powers. She managed to describe the exact contents of substances inside test tubes in just several minutes; something that would take scientists hours to figure out with the use of microscopes and liquid analyses. Biologists, physicists and chemists were involved in the ongoing study of Vera's phenomenal powers. Those scientists saw with their own eyes and reported how she could also change the substances, on a structural level.

After the Bulgarian experiments, Japanese scientists were impressed by Vera and invited her to their country for more large-scale experiments. During their examination of her powers, they were so dumbfounded that they could not believe a human being would be able to achieve such physical results just by using pure energy. The Japanese scientists defined Vera not just as a phenomenon; but as a being that did not belong to the human race. Scientists subjected her to extensive research and tests, which proved that she could change the acidity of water, the levels of alcohol, and even blood pressure in people.

During her sessions, her monitored biological indicators showed that she was in a state of a heart attack. And then again, she always finished the sessions healthy and safe. In fact, if anything, she affected the Japanese testing technology more than it affected her — as it malfunctioned on regular occasions, exposed to her enormous energy levels. At the end of all sessions, Vera rendered plasma-like substance from her mouth in the form of a white cloud. The particle analysis of this substance indicated that it is unknown to science and mankind. Some referred to this plasma-like essence as "prana" as Vera would openly say that this is one of the things she used for healing.

Later on, a Russian neuroscientist would examine her aura with special innovative equipment only found in Russia and a few other countries, as of today. He found out that her energy was so strong that it emanated ultra-bright light from her body, as the brightest part was around her head in the form of a circle — much like how saints are depicted with their halos.

Even though everyone was astonished with her, Vera never took anything for granted; she was never a victim of pride or egocentrism. Her faith in Christ grew even stronger over the years, along with her humility. She would return this attention back to the people and she would always support them in their physical and spiritual battles.

This otherworldly phenomenon remained a woman of her own Bulgarian people, until she died in 2011. Before that she would suffer from many illnesses and had many operations, similarly to most clairvoyants with powers. These powers do come at a price; but their purpose is so much stronger than the suffering itself that the wise soul possessing them can't help but endure and be thankful for that rare chance.

Vera was a very strong and stern woman. Her character was sometimes spiky, as she would openly express her intolerance for evil, hate, aggression and anger. Vera was able to see what real faith could do for you and was sad to observe so many people suffer because they blind themselves to this truth. Vera didn't care that much about science and what the experiments indicated; that wasn't in the essence of true meaning for her. Vera spoke in simple terms, and always became very emotional when it came to the most important things in life — love, laughter, goodness, help, humanity.

Vera Kochovska was here to give us a piece of the afterlife's very essence. However, it was enough to prove to us for the millionth time that the important things remain in the soul, and have nothing to do with material reality. Vera's mission wasn't easy and was probably an unimaginable burden for her. However, she out of all people realised the meaning behind our missions — and she was here also to remind people to follow their unique soul paths, no matter how hard it may seem to be in the here and now. Vera was also destined to pinpoint the spiritual reasons behind each health and vital problem; and this is why she helped with the awakening of so many people, at the cost of her own health and well-being.

THE CHRISTIAN WAY

"Therefore, if anyone is in Christ, he is a new creation. The old has passed away; behold, the new has come." — 2 Corinthians 5:17

These three women are just a few of Bulgaria's bright phenomena. I told you their stories for several crucial reasons.

First of all, I wanted to throw you even deeper into the world of the unconscious. Even though these are extreme cases, it is essential to know that there are people with unlocked potential who have unlimited access to the unconscious territories, as we discussed in the previous chapters. This is why they spoke in symbolic and metaphorical language very often. Their extreme example will help you see clearly the connections between spirit and matter in your own life.

However, by no means try to be like them: they have come on Earth with their own special missions and their own tools for that, and you probably don't share either of those things. They had strange, uncommon lives which were key for the time and for the place they were born into. Don't try to develop or "receive" psychic powers. It is dangerous to break universal laws and achieve powers in an unclean way — powers that you're not designed to have. You already have more than enough to work on, by decoding bits and pieces of your own unconscious realm, and apply the truths to your ultimate awakening.

Secondly, Vanga, Slava and Vera's example will serve to show you how to endure in your own mission after you've decoded your messages. You can learn a lot from them in that respect. They were fragile women, but unyielding fighters, who never complained and walked confidently on their paths cherishing the value of life no matter what. Most of the time it was very difficult and to some people it may even have seemed unbearable. But they knew the cost of giving up, and not giving your best at all times. This is the key of redemption, of cleansing, of achieving your full potential, of deciding to take God's path and not the easy way out.

Don't be afraid to go through fathomless hardships; they do make you stronger and they give you character; they give you a reason to push through even harder, and they give you wisdom. Most of all, they are not empty fights, as they have meaning. In all three women's lives, vital challenges always walked hand in hand with awareness — as they were always able to see the deep underlying meanings of everything. You probably can't literally see those meanings and links, but upon profound introspection you can, and you should, reach this profound truth for your own life purpose and its challenges.

My third reason for describing their stories and powers is to gift you with a glimpse of our true reality. The one that you can't read about in magazines and newspapers, and you can't watch on TV, especially not in mainstream documentaries. All that is merely a distraction from what is truly important. We are all spirits bound inside our temples, called bodies. There is a design for everything, including human souls and their experiences and missions here on earth.

Reality is truly more interesting than any fiction; and you can't capture it all with your five senses. You need to know about the patterns, the structures, and the repeating fractals of our reality — mathematics is the language of God, and it is noticeable in both our micro and macro cosmoses. The three women had exclusive access to all this knowledge, and part of their mission was to share it with the world; with you. Some souls are in a direct link with this other realm, because they have a key purpose here on earth — always born at the right place and time in order to influence the right groups of people, changing human history slightly for the better every time. In your state of transcendence, you have to be aware of such souls and the kind of knowledge they come with and acknowledge them when they enter your life.

The most important reason for me to write about the three women, however, is to emphasise how humble and timid they were. They wouldn't even dare think about gaining profit for what they did; they were only interested in the spiritual progress of the people they interacted with. They made it obvious for everyone how materialism is an "illusion" and made no compromise in vocalising this truth; as this truth was their engine that kept them going, their source of energy and strength. They all had these intrinsic Christian values that would keep them sane and steady throughout their long, difficult and extraordinary lives.

In relation to that, it is not by chance that they were born exactly on Bulgarian lands and had the strong Christian faith inside their hearts. They were almost living in two worlds, and the Christian faith was the thing keeping their minds clear. Vanga, Slava and Vera were walking on the Christian path. They were aware that Jesus was indeed their saviour and were not short on words in their constant prayer and repentance.

"For God gave us a spirit not of fear but of power and love

and self-control." — 2 Timothy 1:7

I need you to know that Christianity in its pure state is the only accurate faith, and I want to be clear on that. Only Christianity informs you that you have already been atoned for your sins even before you were born, because Jesus already died on the cross for you. (There is a lot of symbolism in that too.) Since the Son of God was sacrificed on the cross for you, this was the ultimate proof of God's love and promise for humanity. The only thing that is necessary for you to do now is to be born again. That is, to merely accept Jesus Christ in your heart, as your Lord and Saviour, as the Son of God, and part of the Holy Trinity. If you do that, it will become natural to you to pray and repent, and read the Bible. Keep in mind that only Christianity proposes such a philosophy:

Everything has already been done for you. Evil has ALREADY been defeated. You don't have to do much about it — you just have to accept it and be thankful; and pray. Live a righteous life and repent for your sins. Don't have fear, no matter what comes in life; just get to know God and be in God.

That's it. That's all it takes. No rituals, no strange gatherings and specific types of prayer; no yoga practices, no necessary meditation. Just you, God, and your relationship with Him. Your humility, your repentance, your compassion towards God and all people. Your awareness, your strength and the pure love in your heart, which nobody can take away from you. Your gestures of love and faith in the real world; your acts of spreading the good news to the other souls. Your conscious effort to become a better human every day, getting closer to the image of Christ, which represents perfection.

This is the real Christianity.

This is the real Christian way that has been condemned

for centuries, and people have been killed for it. (Do you think it is a coincidence that such a humble and righteous path has been attacked so much?)

The Christian way is simple and makes total sense when you are awakened to it; that is, when you have been born again. Still, many people refuse to do so, and live in all ways different from the Christian one. Their ego gets in the way. And then Evil joins forces with Ego, and continuously tries to destroy Christianity. But it never will — while it may have corrupted a group of people in lead positions and a couple of churches, Christianity in its pure state is unbreakable, and it doesn't need a building or an institution in order to be true.

There have been a lot of attacks on Christianity recently, there always have been and always will be; this is all part of the trials, and part of the rightful Christian way. But Christianity in its pure form will always remain present, because truth cannot be eradicated. Truth is stronger than all trials on planet Earth combined. Most importantly, the truth will set you free.

The best news is that we all possess a grain of truth inside our hearts — this is your inner compass which easily points you right from wrong. And it overlaps on 100% with the Christian values and the teachings of the Bible.

We need to have a framework to work in accordance with; sometimes trusting our own gut is not enough and we lose our way. Evil gets in the way and affects us, and we question ourselves even in the highest levels of our transcendence state. That is why reading the Bible and understanding its deep underlying meanings reminds us of the Truth, as it easily resonates with our intuition and gets us on the right track again in a matter of seconds.

The Christian way is a giving one. Giving what you have to the person in need is a good enough motivation to keep going. Not because of what you will get by helping them out, but because of what they will get when you help them. It sums up the idea of "It's not about you, it's about them" — a short quote which speaks a thousand words. Still, God is fair, and he will gift you with what you deserve in return:

"Remember this: Whoever sows sparingly will also reap sparingly, and whoever sows generously will also reap generously. Each of you should give what you have decided in your heart to give, not reluctantly or under compulsion, for God loves a cheerful giver. And God is able to bless you abundantly, so that in all things at all times, having all that you need, you will abound in every good work." — 2 Corinthians 9:6-8

Never forget that only Christianity proposes in such a profound way how walking in pain and trials fearlessly will ultimately bring you the sweet fruits of your hard work, if you keep your love of God strong:

"Blessed is the man who remains steadfast under trial, for when he has stood the test, he will receive the crown of life, which God has promised to those who love him." — James 1:12

This is real faith. And it makes you unshakable. It made those three women unshakable too, and this was another reason why they were called "phenomena" — apart from their obvious supernatural powers. Having endured all trials, I am sure they are in a better place now filled with endless bliss and emanating light.

Be aware of those things. Be a seeker after Truth, as now is the time. Employ your state of transcendence into its ultimate function: unyielding faith, which will forever be your shield. Be like the three women in the sense of how intuitively and thirstily they followed Christian faith, and never sacrificed their Christian values.

There is not one single way to build a strong relationship with the Source, but I just hope that with my writing and real stories, I have at least made you think, and feel more deeply, on the Christian topic. I should surely hope so, as only Christ is your way to salvation and only through Christ can you reach the Kingdom of Heaven and be with God, just as it is written in the Bible. There has never been a compromise in that, and there will never be, no matter what some new age religions (or other old religions) make you believe.

"Jesus said to him, 'I am the way, and the truth, and the life; no one comes to the Father but through Me.'" — John 14:6

Giving your life to Christ is no sacrifice. It is actually the ultimate gift you can make for yourself — it gives you freedom of so many things that have bound you before. However, the problem lies in the Ego, and in the fear, superficially caused by the dark side. Fear of the unknown; fear of change; fear of what lies beyond.

This is why, as we've already discussed, fear, and not hatred, is the true polar opposite of love. It has all been staged to be like that; a parade of illusions. And if you still have some fear left, we will eradicate that in our next two chapters called THE HERO'S JOURNEY and NO MORE FEAR — our two last chapters, in which you will gain back your whole strength on 100% and become the superhuman you deserve to be.

THE HERO'S JOURNEY

"Don't be satisfied with stories, how things have gone with others. Unfold your own myth." — Rumi

I want this chapter to be an exclusive present just for you, my dear reader. I want it to be an interactive session; a pure adventure for your soul, and a conversation between you and me in which I guide you through the discovery of the deepest parts of your soul — the ones that you have never shed light on.

I want this chapter to be a challenge posed before you; a push to try out your well-exercised abstract thought and refreshed intuition; a perfect example of the importance of metaphorical expression and its relation to Meaning.

Now is the time to be absolutely transformed, and be the Hero in your life, getting to know your own journey better. Be prepared to observe yourself and your life carefully, to take notes, and to go back and reread or edit chunks of information if necessary. Take this next step to the ladder of Truth and write this chapter of transcendence together with me.

Having studied Carl Jung's work profoundly, I couldn't help but investigate the authors who were influenced by his work too. Joseph Campbell was one of those people: a renowned American professor in literature. He was fascinated with mythology and with Jung's contribution to the investigation of archetypal myth figures and stories. Campbell studied mythology extensively, gathering prototypes from all over the world and comparing them. In his volumetric research, he included many nations, cultures and times in history. It was truly a fascinating investigation.

What he discovered is so archetypical, so applicable to everyone in the course of history, including you, that it has the potential of changing your life right now. He discovered the so-called "monomyth", the original story of almost every myth engraved into the majority of psychés at all times.

It always includes a hero with a special mission. He called that the Hero's Journey, and unveiled the common template behind it, which could be found in most tales and lore around the world. The same template, interestingly enough, could be applied to our modern lives as well, and I dare say, it is more relevant now than ever.

Moreover, his archetypal myth pattern could be used as a great tool for introspection, profound self-reflection and discovery of your very own mission, your very own Hero's Journey, and recognition of all its specific phases. His work is extremely valuable in that respect, as you can utilise it for that purpose continuously in your life, in all its different stages. Laying this template onto your life history so far, as well as onto your prospects for the future, will give you a very rational type of awareness. It will form a structure of your own thoughts and inner realisations; it will immediately explain why you went through this and that trial, and what should come after.

Profound truths tend to come chaotically at times. So Campbell's work is one great way to tame down and organise the ideas that come exclusively from the collective unconscious in the form of archetypal myths. Campbell's pattern will also give you a sense of the types of people (or energies) that will inevitably enter your life, and when to expect them. The knowledge of the monomyth could be your very own self-reflection methodology, your basic way to see your life almost from a third person's perspective, as if you were the author.

Here is a summary of Campbell's monomyth:

A hero ventures forth from the world of common day into a region of supernatural wonder; supernatural forces are there encountered, and a decisive victory is won through a series of trials; the hero then comes back from this mysterious adventure with the power to bestow boons on his fellow man.

You have definitely encountered this pattern in many films and books. But do you already find similarities in your own life? At this point, you must already be aware of your mission (or missions) here on Earth; of your **Hero's Journey**. Please summarise it here:

... ...
... ...
... ...
... ...
... ...

Campbell proposes 17 stages of the monomyth, in his original article from 1949 called *The Hero with a Thousand Faces*. The Hero's journey, according to him, is precisely separated into the following stages:

Departure/Separation:
1. Call to Adventure
2. Refusal of Call
3. Supernatural Aid

4. Crossing First Threshold
5. Belly of the Whale

Initiation:

6. Road of Trials
7. Meeting with the Goddess
8. Temptation
9. Atonement with the Father
10. Apostasis
11. The Ultimate Boon

Return:

12. Refusal of Return
13. The Magic Flight
14. Rescue from Without
15. Crossing the Return Threshold
16. Master of Two Worlds
17. Freedom to Live

Departure:

1. **The Call to Adventure** — the hero begins in a situation of normality from which some information is received that acts as a call to head off into the unknown.

Campbell describes this first stage in *The Hero with a Thousand Faces* in the following way: "... (the call of adventure is) a forest, a kingdom underground, beneath the waves, or above the sky, a secret island, lofty mountain top, or profound dream state; but it is always a place of strangely fluid and polymorphous beings, unimaginable torments, superhuman deeds, and impossible delight. The hero can go forth of their own volition to accomplish the adventure. The adventure may begin as a mere blunder... or still again, one may be only casually strolling when some passing phenomenon catches the wandering eye and lures one away from the frequented paths of man. Examples might be multiplied, ad infinitum, from every corner of the world."

Examples include unlikely heroes such as Frodo Baggins receiving the One Ring from his uncle Bilbo and the wizard Gandalf subsequently asking Frodo to take it from the Shire in *The Fellowship of the Ring*, and Luke Skywalker finding the message of the imperilled Princess Leia in the original *Star Wars* film.

Examples include non-literal Calls to Adventure, like a mere breakthrough idea inside your head, or going into the wilderness of your own intuition for a change. Do you remember how we began?

"At times you have to leave the city of your comfort and go into the wilderness of your intuition. What you'll discover will be wonderful. What you will discover is yourself." — Alan Alda

What was your **Call to Adventure** and why?

... ...
... ...
... ...
... ...
... ...

2. Refusal of the Call — usually when the call is given, the future hero first refuses to act on it. This may be from a sense of duty or obligation to the old world; it is often out of fear, insecurity, a sense of inadequacy, or any reason that works to hold the person in his normal circumstances; in his current comfort zone.

Campbell: "Refusal of the summons converts the adventure into its negative. Walled in boredom, hard work, or 'culture', the subject loses the power of significant affirmative action and becomes a victim to be saved. His flowering world becomes a wasteland of dry stones and his life feels meaningless—even though, like King Minos, he may through titanic effort succeed in building an empire or renown. Whatever house he builds, it will be a house of death: a labyrinth of cyclopean walls to hide from him his minotaur. All he can do is create new problems for himself and await the gradual approach of his disintegration."

After Gandalf tells Frodo he can destroy the One Ring by casting into the fires of Mount Doom in *The Fellowship of the Ring*, Frodo says, "I am not made for perilous quests. I wish I had never seen the Ring! Why did it come to me? Why was I chosen?" Similarly, Luke refuses to join Obi-Wan Kenobi's fight against the Galactic Empire until the empire murders his aunt and uncle.

In real life, it could be any reason why not to go out of your comfort zone and confront your fears. Your own reason not to peek into the Deep and meet with your Shadow, for example.

Have you had an internal **Refusal to your Call**? What was it and why?

... ...
... ...
... ...
... ...
... ...

3. Supernatural Aid — once the hero has committed to the quest, consciously or subconsciously, his guide and magical helper appears or becomes known. More often than not, this supernatural mentor will present the hero with one or more talismans or artifacts, or hidden knowledge, which will aid him later in his quest.

Campbell: "For those who have not refused the call, the first encounter of the hero journey is with a protective figure he is about to pass. What such a figure represents is the benign, protecting power of destiny. The fantasy is a reassurance — promise that the peace of Paradise, which was known first within the mother womb, is not to be lost; that it supports the present and stands in the future as well as in the past (is omega as well as alpha); that though omnipotence may seem to be endangered by the threshold passages and life awakenings, protective power is always and ever present within or just behind the unfamiliar features of the world. One has only to know and trust, and the ageless guardians will appear. Having responded to his own call, and continuing to follow courageously as the consequences unfold, the hero finds all the forces of the unconscious at his side. Mother Nature herself supports the mighty task. And so far as the hero's act coincides with that for which his society is ready, he seems to ride on the great rhythm of the historical process."

The wizard Gandalf and Jedi Master Obi-Wan Kenobi represent the primary mentor in the initial hero's journey cycle.

In real life, there is a little plot twist here. Very often, this wise figure could be God or a messenger of God in your life. It could be the Holy Spirit with yourself, if you listen to it closely. You can even be your own supernatural messenger of light and wisdom, as it happened to me when I found my nine-year-old's writings, went on my quests for truth and immediately started receiving the answers I was looking for from the Source.

What was your **Supernatural Aid** and why?

... ...
... ...
... ...
... ...
... ...

4.   Crossing the First Threshold — the point where the hero actually crosses into the field of adventure, leaving the known limits of his world and venturing into an unknown and dangerous realm where the rules and limits are unknown.

Campbell: "With the personifications of his destiny to

guide and aid him, the hero goes forward in his adventure until he comes to the 'threshold guardian' at the entrance to the zone of magnified power. Such custodians bound the world in four directions — also up and down — standing for the limits of the hero's present sphere, or life horizon. Beyond them is darkness, the unknown and danger; just as beyond the parental watch is danger to the infant and beyond the protection of his society danger to the members of the tribe. The usual person is more than content, he is even proud, to remain within the indicated bounds, and popular belief gives him every reason to fear so much as the first step into the unexplored. The adventure is always and everywhere a passage beyond the veil of the known into the unknown; the powers that watch at the boundary are dangerous; to deal with them is risky; yet for anyone with competence and courage the danger fades."

In *Star Wars*, Tusken Raiders threaten to put an early end to Luke's adventure, and he is further discouraged by his uncle's wishes for him to remain on the farm. When his uncle and aunt are slain by the Empire, he decides to follow in his father's footsteps and learn to become a Jedi.

In real life, this is when you officially step out of your comfort zone and find yourself facing the unknown. It is key to be fearless in this stage, and remember the message bequeathed onto you by the "wise figure".

Describe the **Crossing of the First Threshold** stage in your life:

... ...
... ...
... ...
... ...

5. **Belly of the Whale** — represents the final separation from the hero's known world and self. By entering this stage, the person shows willingness to undergo a metamorphosis. When first entering the stage, the hero may encounter a minor danger or setback.

Campbell: "The idea that the passage of the magical threshold is a transit into a sphere of rebirth is symbolised in the worldwide womb image of the belly of the whale. The hero, instead of conquering or conciliating the power of the threshold, is swallowed into the unknown and would appear to have died. This popular motif gives emphasis to the lesson that the passage of the threshold is a form of self-annihilation. Instead of passing outward, beyond the confines of the visible world, the hero goes inward, to be born again. The disappearance corresponds to the passing of a worshipper into a temple — where he is to be quickened by the recollection of who and what he is, namely dust and ashes unless immortal. The temple interior, the belly of the whale, and the heavenly land beyond, above, and below the confines of the world, are one and the same. That is why the approaches and entrances to temples are flanked and defended by colossal gargoyles: dragons, lions, devil-slayers with drawn swords, resentful dwarfs, winged bulls. The devotee at the moment of entry into a temple undergoes a metamorphosis. Once inside he may be said to have died to time and returned to the World Womb, the World Navel, the Earthly Paradise. Allegorically, then, the passage into a temple and the hero-dive through the jaws of the whale are identical adventures, both denoting in picture language, the life-centring, life-renewing act."

In the exemplary Book of Jonah, the eponymous Israelite refuses God's command to prophesy the destruction of

Nineveh and attempts to flee by sailing to Tarshish. A storm arises, and the sailors cast lots to determine that Jonah is to blame. He allows himself to be thrown overboard to calm the storm and is saved from drowning by being swallowed by a "great fish". Over three days, Jonah commits to God's will, and he is vomited safely onto the shore. He subsequently goes to Nineveh and preaches to its inhabitants. Jonah's passage through the belly of the whale can be viewed as a symbolic death and rebirth in Jungian analysis.

In real life, this is your first test, first trial, assessing how you deal with the difficulties of the unknown and what your reaction will be later on when even harder challenges come.

Describe the **Belly of the Whale** stage in your life, and how you dealt with your first trial:

… …
… …
… …
… …
… …

Initiation:

6. The Road of Trials — a major stage, without which the hero's journey would make no sense. It is a series of tests that the hero must undergo to begin the transformation. Often the hero fails one or more of these tests, which often occur in threes. Eventually the hero will overcome these trials, preparing him for the ultimate battle later on.

Campbell: "Once having traversed the threshold, the hero moves in a dream landscape of curiously fluid, ambiguous forms, where he must survive a succession of trials. This is a favourite phase of the myth-adventure. It has produced a world literature of miraculous tests and ordeals. The hero is covertly aided by the advice, amulets, and secret agents of the supernatural helper whom he met before his entrance into this region. Or it may be that he here discovers for the first time that there is a benign power everywhere supporting him in his superhuman passage. The original departure into the land of trials represented only the beginning of the long and really perilous path of initiatory conquests and moments of illumination. Dragons have now to be slain and surprising barriers passed — again, again, and again. Meanwhile there will be a multitude of preliminary victories, unsustainable ecstasies and momentary glimpses of the wonderful land."

In *The Empire Strikes Back*, the heroes are imperilled by ice monsters, Imperial forces, and an asteroid field before their journeys progress.

In real life, these are the beginnings of your real challenges; and your attitude plays a key role in the way you will overcome them in order to move to the next stage. Here you have to be strong and anticipating, have your guard up at all times, and proceed with a proactive and positive attitude in resolving your problem. There is no "I will try"; you either do it and move on to the next stage, or you don't and you find yourself in a vicious cycle.

Describe your **Road of Trials** stage in your life, and how you dealt with each trial:

… … … … … … … … … … … … … … … … … … …
… … … … … … … … … … … … … … … … … … …
… … … … … … … … … … … … … … … … … … …
… … … … … … … … … … … … … … … … … … …
… … … … … … … … … … … … … … … … … … …

7. The Meeting with the "Goddess" — this is where the hero gains items given to him that will help him in the future. Metaphorically, it could also be a collection of key symbols, prophecies, skills, and other useful teachings. This is the stage in which the triumph of winning all trials leads the hero to meet his opposite energy, which will give him something that he didn't have before.

Campbell: "The ultimate adventure, when all the barriers and ogres have been overcome, is commonly represented as a mystical marriage of the triumphant hero-soul with the Queen Goddess of the World. This is the crisis at the nadir, the zenith, or at the uttermost edge of the earth, at the central point of the cosmos, in the tabernacle of the temple, or within the darkness of the deepest chamber of the heart. The meeting with the goddess (who is incarnate in every woman) is the final test of the talent of the hero to win the boon of love (charity: amor fati), which is life itself enjoyed as the encasement of eternity. And when the adventurer, in this context, is not a youth but a maid, she is the one who, by her qualities, her beauty, or her yearning, is fit to become the consort of an immortal. Then the heavenly husband descends to her and conducts her to his bed — whether she will or not. And if she has shunned him, the scales fall from her eyes; if she has sought him, her desire finds its peace."

In *The Fellowship of the Ring*, Frodo meets the royal Galadriel, who shows him a vision of the future.

In real life, it could be a real person of the opposite sex, who gives you wisdom that you wouldn't be able to attain on your own; thus, the metaphorical "marriage" of the two opposite energies. It could also be the encounter of your own animus and anima (male and female energies, according to

241

Jung), from which hidden pieces of knowledge from your other side swims to the surface for you to utilise in your next challenges.

Who or what was your **Meeting with the Goddess** moment, and what did you gain from that?

... ...
... ...
... ...
... ...

8. **The Temptation** — in this step, the hero faces those temptations, often of a physical or material nature, that may lead him to abandon or stray from his elevated quest. Woman is a metaphor for the physical or material temptations of life, since the hero-knight was often tempted by lust from his spiritual journey. However, it could be anything else pleasurable and intrinsic to the fallen human state like material belongings and comforts, alcohol, food, feasts, distractions.

Campbell: "The crux of the curious difficulty lies in the fact that our conscious views of what life ought to be seldom corresponding to what life really is. Generally, we refuse to admit within ourselves, or within our friends, the fullness of that pushing, self-protective, malodorous, carnivorous, lecherous fever which is the very nature of the organic cell. Rather, we tend to perfume, whitewash, and reinterpret; meanwhile imagining that all the flies in the ointment, all the hairs in the soup, are the faults of some unpleasant someone else. But when it suddenly dawns on us, or is forced to our attention, that everything we think or do is necessarily tainted with the odour of the flesh, then, not uncommonly, there is experienced a moment of revulsion: life, the acts of life, the organs of life, woman in particular as the great symbol of life, become intolerable to the pure, the pure, pure soul... — The seeker of the life beyond life must press beyond (the woman), surpass the temptations of her call, and soar to the immaculate ether beyond."

In *Star Wars*, Luke is beguiled by Leia despite her being his sister. In *The Odyssey*, Calypso tempts Odysseus to stay on the island rather than continuing his journey.

In real life, lust could indeed be the culprit, but not only. It is the general hedonistic way of thinking which we already discussed that keeps too many people at this stage of the journey for years. They fall into the trap of materialistic and physical pleasures, forgetting about their noble mission and what the quest was all about.

What was the **Temptation** moment in your life and why? What did you do to overcome it?

… … … … … … … … … … … … … … … … … … … …
… … … … … … … … … … … … … … … … … … … …
… … … … … … … … … … … … … … … … … … … …
… … … … … … … … … … … … … … … … … … … …
… … … … … … … … … … … … … … … … … … … …

9. Atonement with the Father — in this major step the hero must confront and be initiated by whatever holds the ultimate power in his life. In many myths and stories this is the father, or a father figure who has life and death power. This is the centre point of the journey. All the previous steps have been moving into this place, all that follow will move out from it. Although this step is most frequently symbolised by an encounter with a male entity, it does not have to be a male; just someone or something with an incredible power.

Campbell: "Atonement consists in no more than the abandonment of that self-generated double monster — the dragon thought to be God (superego) and the dragon thought to be Sin (repressed id in Freudian psychoanalysis). But this requires an abandonment of the attachment to ego itself, and that is what is difficult. One must have a faith that the father is merciful, and then a reliance on that mercy. Therewith, the centre of belief is transferred outside of the bedevilling god's tight scaly ring, and the dreadful ogres dissolve. It is in this ordeal that the hero may derive hope and assurance from the helpful female figure, by whose magic (pollen charms or power of intercession) he is protected through all the frightening experiences of the father's ego-shattering initiation. For if it is impossible to trust the terrifying father-face, then one's faith must be centred elsewhere; and with that reliance for support, one endures the crisis — only to find, in the end, that the father and mother reflect each other, and are in essence the same. The problem of the hero going to meet the father is to open his soul beyond terror to such a degree that he will be ripe to understand how the sickening and insane tragedies of this vast and ruthless cosmos are completely validated in the majesty of Being. The hero transcends life with its peculiar blind spot and for a moment rises to a glimpse of the source. He beholds the face of the father, understands — and the two are atoned."

In real life, this step could be interpreted as the realisation of the limits of your ego and the need to give out your life to something bigger, acknowledging the Higher Power and bowing to it; making amends with it. In that you learn that your fear was not justified, and you feel free of it.

Not only fear is resolved like this, but the blessings will come right after. The Father for me represents none other than God, and the sooner you make your atonement with Him, the better. This is the stage of maturity, and of acquiring the real wisdom which you weren't ready for before. This is also the stage in which all necessary doors suddenly open for you.

Have you gone through your **Atonement with the Father** stage in life? How did it feel to shatter your ego and make amends with the Higher Power?

… … … … … … … … … … … … … … … … … … … …
… … … … … … … … … … … … … … … … … … … …
… … … … … … … … … … … … … … … … … … … …
… … … … … … … … … … … … … … … … … … … …

10. Apotheosis — the point of realisation in which a greater understanding is achieved; a rebirth. Armed with this new knowledge and perception, the hero is resolved and ready for the significant part of the adventure — reaching the ultimate goal of the quest.

Campbell: "Those who know, not only that the Everlasting lies in them, but that what they really are is the Everlasting, dwell in the groves of the wish fulfilling trees, drink the brew of immortality, and listen everywhere to the unheard music of eternal concord."

In *The Two Towers*, Gandalf dies after fighting the Balrog and Saruman, and is subsequently resurrected in a new form.

In real life, this is the stage in which you are born again. Literally reborn, after you have accepted Christ in your heart. There is no other feeling like this and whether there are multiple "aha" moments in our lives, the ultimate apotheosis is when we are officially in God.

Only in this way do we find ourselves in the everlasting bliss, here on Earth and later on in the afterlife. The word "apotheosis" itself literally means "the elevation of someone to a divine status" from ancient Greek.

What was your **Apotheosis** in life? What was your divine realisation upon reaching this stage?

... ...
... ...
... ...
... ...
... ...

11. The Ultimate Boon — the achievement of the goal of the quest. It is what the hero went on the journey to get. All the previous steps serve to prepare and purify the hero for this step, since in many myths the boon is something transcendent like the elixir of life itself, or a plant that supplies immortality, or the Holy Grail.

Campbell: "The gods and goddesses then are to be understood as embodiments and custodians of the elixir of Imperishable Being but not themselves the Ultimate in its primary state. What the hero seeks through his intercourse with them is therefore not finally themselves, but their grace, i.e. the power of their sustaining substance. This miraculous energy-substance and this alone is the Imperishable; the names and forms of the deities who everywhere embody, dispense, and represent it come and go. This is the miraculous energy of the thunderbolts of Zeus, Yahweh, and the Supreme Buddha, the fertility of the rain of Viracocha, the virtue announced by the bell rung in the Mass at the consecration, and the light of the ultimate illumination of the saint and sage. Its guardians dare release it only to the duly proven."

This stage is represented by the One Ring being destroyed in *The Return of the King* and the Death Star being destroyed in *Star Wars*.

In real life, this is the achievement of your mission, or one of your missions. It is all hard work and all self-purification combined into this one achieved goal. It also causes you the ultimate moment of bliss; a feeling of being able to achieve anything; a strong confirmation of your beliefs and meanings; a triumph over evil.

This is your ultimate gift that you deserve because you have decided to go out of your comfort zone, go through numerous trials, meet bad and good characters on the way, and purify your soul for the sake of your own Creator. This moment is the very reason you live.

Have you received your **Ultimate Boon** yet? What is it? And if not, what do you think it will be?

... ...
... ...
... ...
... ...
... ...

Return:

12. Refusal of the Return — having found bliss and enlightenment in the other world, the hero may not want to return to the ordinary world to bestow the boon onto his fellow man.

Campbell: "When the hero-quest has been accomplished,

through penetration to the source, or through the grace of some male or female, human or animal, personification, the adventurer still must return with his life-transmuting trophy. The full round, the norm of the monomyth, requires that the hero shall now begin the labour of bringing the runes of wisdom, the Golden Fleece, or his sleeping princess, back into the kingdom of humanity, where the boon may redound to the renewing of the community, the nation, the planet or the ten thousand worlds. But the responsibility has been frequently refused. Even Gautama Buddha, after his triumph, doubted whether the message of realisation could be communicated, and saints are reported to have died while in supernal ecstasy. Numerous indeed are the heroes fabled to have taken up residence forever in the blessed isle of the unageing Goddess of Immortal Being."

After destroying the ring, Frodo is so exhausted he wants to give up and die rather than make the return journey, but he has to for the sake of his people — it is part of his journey.

In real life, this stage like the majority of others is more metaphorical than anything else. Some people completely refuse the material ways having come into contact with the divine side, and the eternal bliss of extrasensory existence. The enlightenment makes it difficult to get back to where you started, and you might prefer to stay in the space which lacks time or petty human rules.

However, there is a reason why we live in this physical existence, and not in the spiritual world yet. The material reality should not be completely sacrificed yet. You have to descend back to the normal living with new awareness, which you must pass onto your fellow brothers and sisters, as opposed to keeping this exclusive knowledge to yourself.

Do you think you will have a **Refusal to your Return**, and why? Has this already happened to you, and when?

... ...
... ...
... ...
... ...
... ...

13. The Magic Flight — sometimes the hero must escape with the boon, if it is something that the "gods" have been jealously guarding. It can be just as adventurous and dangerous returning from the journey as it was to go on it.

Campbell: "If the hero in his triumph wins the blessing of the goddess or the god and is then explicitly commissioned to return to the world with some elixir for the restoration of society, the final stage of his adventure is supported by all the powers of his supernatural patron. On the other hand, if the trophy has been attained against the opposition of its guardian, or if the hero's wish to return to the world has been resented by the gods or demons, then the last stage of the mythological round becomes a lively, often comical, pursuit. This flight may be complicated by marvels of magical obstruction and evasion."

Frodo and his companion are rescued by giant eagles on their way back to the Shire.

In real life, this is when you should be very wary of dark presence and dark forces. What you will have is the eternal truth within you, so this is when you will get attacks from the Shadows the most. Evil doesn't want you to bestow peace amongst people with this hero knowledge that you possess, so it will try its best to obstruct you on your way back to the people.

Have you had your **Magic Flight**? Describe it here. If not, what do you think the obstruction during the "flight" back would be?

… … … … … … … … … … … … … … … … … … … …
… … … … … … … … … … … … … … … … … … … …
… … … … … … … … … … … … … … … … … … … …
… … … … … … … … … … … … … … … … … … … …
… … … … … … … … … … … … … … … … … … …

14. Rescue from Without — just as the hero may need guides and assistants to set out on the quest, often he must have powerful guides and rescuers to bring him back to everyday life, especially if the person has been wounded or weakened by the experience.

Campbell: "The hero may have to be brought back from his supernatural adventure by assistance from without. That is to say, the world may have to come and get him. For the bliss of the deep abode is not lightly abandoned in favour of the self-scattering of the wakened state. 'Who having cast off the world,' we read, 'would desire to return again? He would be only there.' And yet, in so far as one is alive, life will call. Society is jealous of those who remain away from it and will come knocking at the door. If the hero... is unwilling, the disturber suffers an ugly shock; but on the other hand, if the summoned one is only delayed — sealed in by the beatitude of the state of perfect being (which resembles death) — an apparent rescue is affected, and the adventurer returns."

When Frodo is tempted to keep the One Ring rather than destroy it at Mount Doom, Gollum takes it from him, unwittingly ensuring its destruction. At the end of the original *Star Wars* film, Han Solo returns in the Millennium Falcon to defend Luke so he can destroy the Death Star.

In real life, this is more of a game of chances, synchronicities and divine intervention. Being helped from the outside at the right moment might seem like "pure luck" but in reality, calculated miracles are also a part of the equation. Help could come from another person that "randomly" arrives just in time for the rescue; or a divine intervention happens and the Holy Spirit within you reminds you who you are, despite the constant evil attacks on your way back.

Have you had your **Rescue from Without** moment? Describe it here. If not, where do you think your "lucky" save will come from?

... ...
... ...
... ...
... ...
... ...

15. The Crossing of the Return Threshold — the moment when the hero enters back into his old realm of existence, beliefs, traditions; his previous small comfort zone. The place is the same, but the journey has changed him tremendously, along with his view of this place. According to Campbell, "The returning hero, to complete his adventure, must survive the impact of the world." The trick in returning is to retain the wisdom gained on the quest, to integrate that wisdom into a human life, and then figure out how to share the wisdom with the rest of the world.

Campbell: "Many failures attest to the difficulties of this life-affirmative threshold. The first problem of the returning hero is to accept as real, after an experience of the soul-satisfying vision of fulfilment, the passing joys and sorrows, banalities and noisy obscenities of life. Why re-enter such a world? Why attempt to make plausible, or even interesting, to men and women consumed with passion, the experience of transcendental bliss? As dreams that were momentous by night may seem simply silly in the light of day, so the poet and the prophet can discover themselves playing the idiot before a jury of sober eyes. The easy thing is to commit the whole community to the devil and retire again into the heavenly rock dwelling, close the door, and make it fast. But if some spiritual obstetrician has drawn the shimenawa across the retreat, then the work of representing eternity in time, and perceiving in time eternity, cannot be avoided."

In the penultimate chapter of *The Lord of the Rings*, the hobbits confront and must defeat Saruman in the Shire before things can return to normal.

In real life, this is your chance to lead your final battle and then take a breath and find yourself in peace. You now have the chance to compare your life to what it was before and see how far you've come. The past seems still, colourless, and uninteresting now, and your previous comfort zone seems way too small. You will have to adapt back to your old place, but not to your old ways. You have to retain the wisdom achieved on the way and apply it to your everyday life and the lives of others.

Have you had your **Crossing of the Return Threshold** moment? Describe it here. If not, what do you think the comparison between your life before and after the journey will look like? What are you going to do to share your exclusive knowledge with the world after your return?

… … … … … … … … … … … … … … … … … …
… … … … … … … … … … … … … … … … … …
… … … … … … … … … … … … … … … … … …
… … … … … … … … … … … … … … … … … …
… … … … … … … … … … … … … … … … … …

16. **Master of Two Worlds** — this means achieving the ultimate balance between the material and spiritual. The hero has become comfortable and competent in both the inner and outer worlds.

Campbell: "Freedom to pass back and forth across the world division, from the perspective of the apparitions of time to that of the causal deep and back — not contaminating the principles of the one with those of the other, yet permitting the mind to know the one by virtue of the other — is the talent of the master. The Cosmic Dancer, declares Nietzsche, does not rest heavily in a single spot, but gaily, lightly, turns and leaps from one position to another. It is possible to speak from only one point at a time, but that does not invalidate the insights of the rest. The individual, through prolonged psychological disciplines, gives up completely all attachment to his personal limitations, idiosyncrasies, hopes and fears, no longer resists the self- annihilation that is prerequisite to rebirth in the realisation of truth, and so becomes ripe, at last, for the great atonement. His personal ambitions being totally dissolved, he no longer tries to live but willingly relaxes to whatever may come to pass in him; he becomes, that is to say, an anonymity."

By the time of *Return of the Jedi*, Luke has become a Jedi

knight. Former Jedi knight Anakin Skywalker sheds his alter ego as the Sith lord Darth Vader when he throws down the Emperor, and, moreover, returns as a Force spirit after his death.

This is the moment in which you achieve the perfect balance and you do not need confirmation from your ego for that. Ego has already been shattered and you do not search for fame. The mere understanding of the duality of our existence is a good enough of a gift for you because you can now freely live in both worlds. You have been enlightened and life will never be the same. Living in peace is what is expected for you from this point on.

Have you had the **Master of Two Worlds** state? Describe it here. If not, how do you think you will feel upon reaching this profound state?

... ...
... ...
... ...
... ...
... ...

17. **Freedom to Live** — in this last step, mastery leads to freedom from the fear of death, which in turn is the freedom to live. This is sometimes referred to as living in the moment, neither anticipating the future nor regretting the past.

Campbell: "The hero is the champion of things becoming, not of things become, because he is. 'Before Abraham was, I AM.' He does not mistake apparent changelessness in time for the permanence of Being, nor is he fearful of the next moment (or of the 'other thing'), as destroying the permanent with its change. 'Nothing retains its own form; but Nature, the greater renewer, ever makes up forms from forms. Be sure that nothing perishes in the whole universe; it does but vary and renew its form.' Thus, the next moment is permitted to come to pass."

In *The Return of the King*, the peaceful resolution is illustrated by the hobbits prospering in their homeland, while Gandalf and Frodo sail to the Undying Lands.

In real life, this is your ultimate gift of peace for years to come, until another call for adventure becomes a necessity. However, there will be no more fear, as you will have already learned the importance of adaptivity and change. Change is the only constant. And appreciating every present moment of life without a rush makes it all the more pleasurable, and easier.

Have you experienced the **Freedom to Live** after fulfilling your mission? Describe it here. If not, why do you think it is important at this last stage to live in the moment, and fully accept change without fear?

… … … … … … … … … … … … … … … … … … …
… … … … … … … … … … … … … … … … … … …
… … … … … … … … … … … … … … … … … … …
… … … … … … … … … … … … … … … … … … …
… … … … … … … … … … … … … … … … … … …

***

Having gone through the phases of the Hero's Journey, I hope that you have reached some profound realisations about your own metaphorical or literal quests. Additionally, I hope that you have discovered how strong you were in certain moments of trial, and how your nature was the one of a hero.

Don't forget that this state doesn't have to be momentary. You can regain the control of your own book of life and write the best story for your protagonist — yourself. The key is to always give out your best as an author, and not just in key moments, until your protagonist fulfils all his missions. Don't skip chapters; you wouldn't be able to anyway. Only in this way will you be able to turn your real life into a hero's masterpiece.

In reality, the Hero's Journey is not one single mission, but a series of missions that need to be fulfilled in the course of a lifetime. Usually, the quests come in cycles, and one must always be aware of the peculiar manifestations of the first step — Call to Adventure. Everything else will depend on you from then on, and on the choices you make at each stage. You can even try applying this new knowledge to the lives of your friends, family, spouse, colleagues, fictional characters, my own stories described in this book — it will always ring true.

I will leave you those few lines to write your general impressions and realisations of that Hero's Journey framework for self-awareness and introspection. How do you feel after this experiment?

… …
… …
… …
… …
… …

Bear in mind that sometimes you will fall back to previous stages until you get it right, and maybe this has already happened to you. But regardless of that, the important thing to remember from Campbell and his extensive research is to never fear, as everything somehow always falls into its place if you are doing the right things.

We shall look into that in our last chapter, NO MORE FEAR which should eliminate your smallest remnants of unproductive fear that might still keep you anxious about embarking on your quest or reaching the next stage of your profound awakening.

NO MORE FEAR
... or how to make a difference

"Do not be anxious about anything, but in everything by prayer and supplication with thanksgiving let your requests be made known to God. And the peace of God, which surpasses all understanding, will guard your hearts and your minds in Christ Jesus. Finally, brothers, whatever is true, whatever is honourable, whatever is just, whatever is pure, whatever is lovely, whatever is commendable, if there is any excellence, if there is anything worthy of praise, think about these things."
— Philippians 4:6-8

You have already gone through a lot. I am proud of you. You know you have already been a hero multiple times in your life. And you know that you can make it possible to sustain this state in the long run. Your desire to be awakened has helped you in assessing every part of your life and vital choices, your behaviours, and your shadow manifestations. Your life seems less chaotic and sounder.

You have learned the importance of helping people and what that means for the growth of your own soul. You know how vital it is to make conscious effort to be better, and to be humble. You have learned about the pricey cost of "loving" yourself just the way you are, without striving to become a better human being. You have mastered, or are in the process of mastering, the art of introspection and of finding the Truth within. You know that mistakes and challenges are not setbacks, but adventures designed to enrich your soul. In your process of getting in tune with your Inner Self and the Higher Power, you understand the importance of asking questions.

This is your balance achieved. First phase of your Awakening Ignited.

You are now aware that happiness is a choice, and not a reaction to external events. Strength of character is too. You already start to think in terms of "energies" and not in terms of "things". You build your relationship with God, and the Voice in you gets stronger and clearer.

You don't have the need to prove yourself to anybody; you are just doing your own thing. You also know how essential it is to be in the right company — your kindred spirits — as this is indispensable and incomparable to anything. You have assessed and strengthened your right relationships and have let go of the wrong ones. Hopefully, you have even met your soulmate, or are in the process of meeting them in the near future. Always remember that your unyielding faith and prayer will definitely get you there, once you have achieved your balance.

Furthermore, you are now completely aware of your transformations for the better and could follow through with them in real time. You are so awakened to your inner state at this point that even the slightest change is measurable. Together with your loved one, the right One, you are aware that you can achieve anything. You are actively working towards your mission and self-reflect with each change, and on each step.

This is your transformation achieved. Second phase of your Awakening Ignited.

Having reached your transcendence state, the language of

the unconscious becomes your everyday code to meaning happiness and success. You clearly see mainstream science's true nature: a flawed instrument of scarce knowledge used for mass manipulation. The Voice within you, however, has become your greatest ally and trusted friend. You now understand metaphors, symbolism, and myths better than ever, and how to apply them into your own Hero's Journey. The energies that seemed vague and inexplicable before have now become part of your daily life. This is why synchronicities and miracles no longer seem otherworldly but serve as real signs of divine guidance.

You are uncompromisingly kind and helpful to people; and you have a noteworthy composure which makes you stand out from all the shaken, overly emotional and dramatic people. They have probably asked you once or twice already what you do differently to be this calm and balance. You know your basic answer is that you are an unyielding believer in God, and this gives you strong roots. You are interested in teaching others of what you have learned. At this point, you are also interested in making even the finer details perfect.

Your last stage in transcendence is to learn how to let go of fear. Completely.

Your trust in God is directly related to that. Once you give your life to Christ, you gradually let go of all negativity, which is always a product of fear. Fear, being the opposite of love, has many manifestations. And unless you give out your life to Christ completely, and make yourself free, you will always have those little bugs of tension, insecurity, worry or doubt. You also see them clearly and more strongly manifested in other people, especially in those who state that they "don't need God in their lives in order to be happy". You have already worked on your Shadow and you know very well the truth behind that. So hopefully you have removed the big chunks of fear and all its major manifestations from your soul. Now is the time to work on the residual particles.

Take worry, for example. This is probably the most common culprit for people's lack of complete happiness. Rationally, we can always state that worry is unnecessary — it would never change anything, it could only make things worse. It's logical. However, thinking about it logically will not make worry go away in an instant. It is not how our systems work. Rationality is never enough; this is why "rational" people and atheistic followers of materialistic mainstream science are rarely truly happy. We need to have a deep understanding and profound insight of what worry really is, where it came from and what we have to do to remove it.

We need to dissect it and study it in our mind laboratory.

Worry, in its essence, is just an intrusive thought. It comes uninvited. We can use the so-called Mindfulness technique to observe it. This means "looking" at the thought from the third person's perspective; we examine it as a separate fragment, disconnected from our whole system. We study it for what it is — just a weak parasite which can't live for long on its own, when we detach it. We see that worry is a subspecies of fear, which in its essence is fed by Evil, and its natural habitat is in the Shadow.

Fear is useful only when there is a life threat. Worry is not useful for anything, as there is never a direct life threat in front of you. Worry is a residual particle of your subconscious attempt to be in absolute control. It is the residual particle of your disbelief that God always prepares the best for you, and He is the one in absolute control.

In that sense, letting go of worry means trusting God completely, with your whole being. He always knows what's useful for you, from the perspective of the Greater good. This is why letting go of fear completely comes only after you have achieved great maturity and wisdom. It has nothing to do with age. You can be very old and experienced, and still not mature and wise enough in that respect. It takes to be a wise sage, to understand that even bad things in life happen for the sake of the Greater good for your own soul, and for the "pilgrim's progress" of the whole of humanity.

Worry keeps you from getting to the next level. Moving forward sometimes means to give in to the problems and bad emotions that come into your life right now. You have to go through them boldly with strength and patience, and definitely without worry — just like in the Hero's Journey. You need to persist no matter what. It's healthy to "go with the flow" every now and then. Because you know in your heart of hearts that everything was designed to be just this way, and there was no mistake. All that is required from you is to actively work through it and expect the sunrise to come right after.

"... but the one who stands firm to the end will be saved." — Matthew 24:13

Letting go of worry means replacing it with thankfulness.

Be thankful for the challenges that have come or will come into your life, against all odds. You were taught to worry when an obstacle comes as they told you it's the natural and "normal" reaction. But it isn't. Being thankful for the new challenge relieves you from fear, as you no longer give it strength.

You thus cut the cord of fear before it has reached your soul and has found its residence in your Shadow. You choose what to give power to. The problem itself? Or your arsenal of strengths? The problem is just one, but you have this variety of weapons that could spiritually annihilate it in a second, before you have dealt with it in the material reality.

Your weapons include: thankfulness, love, endurance, composure, patience, kindness, forgiveness, hope, and most importantly, complete faith in God and his plan for you.

Choose to take it spiritually; choose to take it as a game. When you roll the dice and an undesirable result appears, decide to be happy about it nonetheless — even just for the fun of it. Just because you can, and you know you can. This will ultimately help you win the game more than the odds of the dice.

Even better, choose to take it as making art. You paint the colours of your events yourself; you are the artist. They are colourless in themselves. Nobody can tell you what the right way to react is and what colours to use for your own painting. Reacting with thankfulness is the healthiest and wisest way of all, and a promise of a great art masterpiece. It is also a promise of eliminating even the tiniest remnants of fear.

"It all depends on how we look at things, and not how they are in themselves." — C.G. Jung

We can apply the same exact rule for how you react to standard, "normal" things in life. And behold, this is your ultimate key to complete happiness:

You react with the deepest thankfulness and passion that you can find in your heart. You paint common events in beautiful colours, and you take the time to appreciate them deeply — just like when you see a wonderful masterpiece with your favourite shades. You paint your appreciation into the smallest events, and life smiles back at you more beautiful than ever.

For example, take the time to appreciate the beautiful sunset and how it makes you feel. Or that coffee you just bought from a new place that tastes surprisingly good. Or that beautiful song that gives you chills and leaves you in an inspired mood. Or the few seconds of a stranger smiling back at you — those instances stuck in time, which hold a special beauty only for you to witness.

Don't be a soulless consumer, and let go of your materialistic expectations. Nobody owes you anything. And yet, God has created all of this for you, and has sacrificed his only Son to release you from your sins.

Never take anything for granted, and be thankful even for the most basic things — like the fact that your eyes are healthy enough to read this book right now, or that you have a place to sleep tonight. Be appreciative of your food and think about the process it went through before getting in your mouth. Appreciate good art and all the finer details of a product, considering the time and effort of the artist to get it on this level. Avoid being a harsh critic before you have escaped your ego and explore the product with deep understanding and insight.

Be like that with people as well. Don't judge. Always come from a perspective of deep understanding and insight and forget about forcefully asserting your own beliefs to someone else's life and journey. Nobody owes you anything. But you can learn a lot from everyone, and you could potentially help anyone.

Can you see how thankfulness and appreciation directly leads you to a very humble state? They lead you away from unhealthy ego, superficiality, and beastly consumerism. All divine qualities are connected, and deeply rooted in the original one: love.

"But the fruit of the Spirit is love, joy, peace, patience, kindness, goodness, faithfulness..." — Galatians 5:22

God made our world with love; and this is our natural state. Good thing that love has many manifestations as well; it's not just fear that branches out. You already know what those varieties of love are; you just need to practise them in your daily life in order to win the game of life, learn your lesson, and be in absolute bliss.

Being deprived of fear means living in constant love.

There is no place for fear in the hearts of the people who are overflowing with divine love. Love, in that sense, is directly related to awareness and knowledge, and to the trust that God takes care of us no matter what comes on this material plane. In that sense, overflowing with love is a sign of your deepest, most core awakening.

Upon reaching this state in transcendence, you don't limit yourself to the sources of love (knowledge, awakening, faith) that come into your life. Even the smallest flower that seems insignificant to others is a source of Divine love for you. And your travel to another country becomes a deep spiritual journey, as opposed to just another holiday.

You stop wasting your time with meaningless things, as your focus is on the Light now, while everything else has become a distraction or a background noise. The new trend of clothing or technology holds no importance anymore, and you feel repulsed by celebrity gossip. You appreciate your time now more than ever, and you employ it only in accordance with your mission, without many distractions.

Love makes the Voice in you louder and clearer, and

suddenly everything seems simple. You learn to recognise manifestations of love in everything and everyone. Just as you learn to recognise fear in everything and everyone. You know people now more than ever. And you can't help but feel repulsed by some people who lack love in their lives and their behaviours. You literally sense their insecurities and manifestations of black fear in real time. You have been there, and you know what they need to do in order to recover and heal. You might feel the need to change them, to give them what you have and what you have learned. It's this stage of the Hero's Journey which urges you to bestow the ultimate boon to your fellow men. However, be careful and don't be hasty; assess how ready they are first.

The only rule about this is to never limit the love you share; you have it overflowing anyway. Always stay uncompromisingly kind and gentle, as this is what real strength and real love means.

"And the Lord's servant must not be quarrelsome but kind to everyone, able to teach, patiently enduring evil." — 2 Timothy 2:24

Be patient with people and their journeys. Everyone has their own pace of learning in the school of life. But if you continuously give them the fruits of love at all times, sooner or later they will learn; it is inevitable.

The reason why it is difficult for so many people to adapt to the Light in an instant is that they have to relearn what it's like to live in love. Evil has done a lot of efforts over the years to lure us away from the light; to manipulate us into thinking that fear is our natural habitat. Thus, the majority of souls forget where they came from and where they are headed. They forget their real Creator and the truth about this superficial temporary material reality. So it takes time for them to adjust and get in tune with their real being. Forgive them and be patient with them.

Think about the others' wellbeing and don't judge them. Everyone has a different journey and a different original design. Help whomever you can, whenever you can. Choose not to be egotistical, against all popular trends about that. Don't be greedy to get more and more for yourself; a pleasure thief, only capable of destruction. Live to help others and yourself grow, as this is evergreen and ever true; and always a path to creation rather than destruction. Employ your freshly achieved mindset into helpful words and actions. Don't lock it in yourself.

"The thief comes only to steal and kill and destroy. I came that THEY may have life and have it abundantly." — John 10:10

Last but not least, learn how to be a master of both worlds which will give you the ultimate freedom to live — the last stages of your Hero's Journey. Don't sacrifice the physical just yet. You have a reason to reside in the material. As much as the spiritual is alluring and far more intriguing, you still have these physical boundaries that you shouldn't strive to overcome. They are your necessary anchors.

However, you need to employ your spiritual knowledge into everything you do here on this plane. Never forget who you are and what your true reality is. Find the underlying meaning behind everything, and never stop your seeking process. Only in this way will your awakening make sense. Only in this way will you be successful in completing your Hero's Journey.

"Therefore, if you have been raised up with Christ, keep

seeking the things above, where Christ is, seated at the right hand of God." — Colossians 3:1

***

Your awakening is now fully ignited. Congratulations. How are you feeling?

I hope that this book gave you a lot of the answers you needed just for this exact stage of your life. This was its ultimate purpose:

"...which things we also speak, not in words taught by human wisdom, but in those taught by the Spirit, combining spiritual thoughts with spiritual words." — 1 Corinthians 2:13

New questions will always emerge. However, you have the recipe to obtain even more knowledge now. I am not asking you to believe in anything I've written; I am urging you to test everything and discover the Truth within yourself and in the Holy Bible, without much additional reading. I am sure that the Voice within you has already resonated with the majority of my writing anyway; however, "testing never hurts", does it?

With this book I managed to fulfil one of my missions. This is a dream come true moment for me — to finally finish my writing and publish it for people to see. The path of my maturity has led me to not only reach the Truth in the course of my challenges, but to share it with my fellow men too.

The thirst for intuitive expression has been quenched. I have now externalised my deepest knowledge of the awakening process and have summarised it into a very simple three-phased structure: balance, transformation, transcendence. A basic composition that always rings true for all ages, nations, and types of people.

I hope that you have sensed the peculiarity and feeble magic of the Balkan spirit in my writing. I could never cheat on my Bulgarian nature, as this is a big part of me and my unconscious pool of collective knowledge and truths. The ancient Bulgarian spirit is a strong one; and for some reason has always led us Bulgarians into the right moral direction, against all odds, enlightening many other peoples and nations on the way.

In this regard, I hope that you have also understood the importance of asserting the right moral and traditional values into your art product. We all have to choose our battles, yes, but the law of creation requires us all to make the right type of art without any compromise. People should surround themselves with goodness and truth, and not meaningless kitsch, to put it lightly. Have this in mind in your own inspiration to create and preserve.

During my continuous writing and editing, I received advice from multiple sources not to share my intimate personal experience and life events. However, I never cheated on my intuition, and I didn't listen to this advice.

I have always strived to be ultimately open, honest, and real; I have worked towards my authenticity. So what you received from this book was a very raw, organic material of my own journey so far.

Of course, I am still crossing paths with kindred spirits, and enemies getting into new adventures and myths. I am still, in a way, writing the story of the two boys and the castle. I am by no means a finished book; as my life begins always now. And I am writing my new chapters with faith and love.

Today is a new chapter in my life. This book is getting more and more interesting. Today is a new chapter for you too.

Never forget that.

I am honoured to have provided you this reading material, and to be part of your journey.

It doesn't have to end here. Feel free to reach me for more deep, spiritual, psychological, or purely scientific discussions.

Sincerely Yours,

R.P. Heaven

RPHeavenBooks@gmail.com

"The end of something is better than its beginning. Patience is better than pride." — Ecclesiastes 7:8